Andrew L. Simon:

THE COLLEGE RACKET

Foreword by

Charlton Heston

Edited by

Diana Amsden

ISBN: 1-931313-12-1

Library of Congress Catalog Card Number: 99-90325

Distributed by Ingram Book Company

Printed by Lightning Source Inc. La Vergne, TN 37086

Published by Simon Publications, P. O. Box 321, Safety Harbor, FL 34695-0321

Contents

Foreword

Charlton Heston:

Winning the Cultural War

I remember my son when he was five, explaining to his kindergarten class what his father did for a living.

"My Daddy," he said, "pretends to be people."

There have been quite a few of them. Prophets from the Old and New Testaments, a couple of Christian saints, generals of various nationalities and different centuries, several kings, three American presidents, a French cardinal and two geniuses, including Michelangelo. If you want the ceiling re-painted I'll do my best. There always seem to be a lot of different fellows up here. I m never sure which one of them gets to talk. Right now, I guess I'm the guy.

As I pondered our visit tonight it struck me: If my Creator gave me the gift to connect you with the hearts and minds of those great men, then I want to use that same gift now to re-connect you with your own sense of liberty your own freedom of thought ... your own compass for what is right.

Dedicating the memorial at Gettysburg, Abraham Lincoln said of America, "We are now engaged in a great Civil War, testing whether this nation or any nation so conceived and so dedicated can long endure."

Those words are true again. I believe that we are again engaged in a great civil war, a cultural war that's about to hijack your birthright to think and say what resides in your heart. I fear you no longer trust the pulsing lifeblood of liberty inside you ... the stuff that made this country rise from wilderness into the miracle that it is.

Let me back up. About a year ago I became president of the National Rifle Association, which protects the right to keep and bear arms. I ran for office, I was elected, and now I serve ... I serve as a moving target for the media who've called me everything from "ridiculous" and "duped" to a "brain-injured, senile, crazy old man." I know ... I'm pretty old... but I sure Lord ain't senile.

As I have stood in the cross hairs of those who target Second Amendment freedoms, I've realized that firearms are not the only issue. No, it's much, much bigger than that.

I've come to understand that a cultural war is raging across our land, in which, with Orwellian fervor, certain acceptable thoughts and speech are mandated.

For example, I marched for civil rights with Dr. King in 1963—long before Hollywood found it fashionable. But when I told an audience last year that white pride is just as valid as black pride or red pride or anyone else's pride, they called me a racist.

I've worked with brilliantly talented homosexuals all my life. But when I told an audience that gay rights should extend no further than your rights or my rights, I was called a homophobe.

I served in World War II against the Axis powers. But during a speech, when I drew an analogy between singling out innocent Jews and singling out innocent gun owners, I was called an anti-Semite.

Everyone I know knows I would never raise a closed fist against my country. But when I asked an audience to oppose this cultural persecution, I was compared to Timothy McVeigh.

From Time magazine to friends and colleagues, they're essentially saying, "Chuck, how dare you speak your mind. You are using language not authorized for public consumption!"

But I am not afraid. If Americans believed in political correctness, we'd still be King George's boys—subjects bound to the British crown.

In his book, "*The End of Sanity*," Martin Gross writes that "blatantly irrational behavior is rapidly being established as the norm in almost every area of human endeavor. There seem to be new customs, new rules, new anti-intellectual theories regularly foisted on us from every direction. Underneath, the nation is roiling. Americans know something without a name is undermining the nation, turning the mind mushy when it comes to separating truth from falsehood and right from wrong. And they don't like it."

Let me give a few examples. At Antioch College in Ohio, young men seeking intimacy with a coed must get verbal permission at each step of the process from kissing to petting to final copulation ... all clearly spelled out in a printed college directive.

In New Jersey, despite the death of several patients nationwide who had been infected by dentists who had concealed their AIDs—the state commissioner announced that health providers who are HIV-positive need not ... need not ... tell their patients that they are infected.

At William and Mary, students tried to change the name of the school team "The Tribe" because it was supposedly insulting to local Indians, only to learn that authentic Virginia chiefs truly like the name.

In San Francisco, city fathers passed an ordinance protecting the rights of transvestites to cross-dress on the job, and for transsexuals to have separate toilet facilities while undergoing sex change surgery.

In New York City, kids who don't speak a word of Spanish have been placed in bilingual classes to learn their three R's in Spanish solely because their last names sound Hispanic.

At the University of Pennsylvania, in a state where thousands died at Gettysburg opposing slavery, the president of that college officially set up segregated dormitory space for black students.

Yeah, I know ... that's out of bounds now. Dr. King said "Negroes." Jimmy Baldwin and most of us on the March said "black." But it's a no-no now. For me, hyphenated identities are awkward ... particularly "Native-American." I'm a Native American, for God's sake. I also happen to be a blood-initiated brother of the Miniconjou Sioux. On my wife's side, my grandson is a thirteenth generation native American ... with a capital letter on '"American."

Finally, just last month ... David Howard, head of the Washington D.C. Office of Public Advocate, used the word "niggardly" while talking to colleagues about budgetary matters. Of course, "niggardly" means stingy or scanty. But within days Howard was forced to publicly apologize and resign.

As columnist Tony Snow wrote: "David Howard got fired because some people in public employ were morons who (a) didn't know the meaning of niggardly, (b) didn't know how to use a dictionary to discover the meaning, and (c) actually demanded that he apologize for their ignorance."

What does all of this mean? It means that telling us what to think has evolved into telling us what to say, so telling us what to do can't be far behind.

Before you claim to be a champion of free thought, tell me: Why did political correctness originate on America's campuses? And why do you continue to tolerate it? Why do you, who're supposed to debate ideas, surrender to their suppression?

Let's be honest. Who here thinks your professors can say what they really believe?

It scares me to death, and should scare you too, that the superstition of political correctness rules the halls of reason.

You are the best and the brightest. You, here in the fertile cradle of American academia, here in the castle of learning on the Charles River, you are the cream. But I submit that you, and your counterparts across the land, are the most socially conformed and politically silenced generation since Concord Bridge.

And as long as you validate that ... and abide it ... you are—by your grandfathers standards—cowards.

Here's another example. Right now at more than one major university, Second Amendment scholars and researchers are being told to shut up about their findings or they'll lose their jobs. Why? Because their research findings would undermine big-city mayors' pending lawsuits that seek to extort hundreds of millions of dollars from firearm manufacturers.

I don't care what you think about guns. But if you are not shocked at that, I am shocked at you. Who will guard the raw material of unfettered ideas, if not you? Who will defend the core value of academia, if you supposed soldiers of free thought and expression lay down your arms and plead, "Don't shoot me."

If you talk about race, it does not make you a racist. If you see distinctions between the genders, it does not make you a sexist. If you think critically about a denomination, it does not make you anti-religion. If you accept but don't celebrate homosexuality, it does not make you a homophobe. .

Don't let America's universities continue to serve as incubators for this rampant epidemic of new McCarthyism.

But what can you do? How can anyone prevail against such pervasive social subjugation?

The answer's been here all along. I learned it 36 years ago, on the steps of the Lincoln Memorial in Washington D.C., standing with Dr. Martin Luther King and two hundred thousand people.

You simply ... disobey. Peaceably, yes. Respectfully, of course. Nonviolently, absolutely. But when told how to think or what to say or how to behave, we don't. We disobey social protocol that stifles and stigmatizes personal freedom.

I learned the awesome power of disobedience from Dr. King ... who learned it from Gandhi, and Thoreau, and Jesus, and every other great man who led those in the right against those with the might.

Disobedience is in our DNA. We feel innate kinship with that disobedient spirit that tossed tea into Boston Harbor, that sent Thoreau to jail, that refused to sit in the back of the bus, that protested a war in Viet Nam.

In that same spirit, I am asking you to disavow cultural correctness with massive disobedience of rogue authority, social directives and onerous laws that weaken personal freedom.

But be careful ... it hurts. Disobedience demands that you put yourself at risk. Dr. King stood on lots of balconies. You must be willing to be humiliated ... to endure the modern-day equivalent of the police dogs at Montgomery and the water cannons at Selma.

You must be willing to experience discomfort. I m not complaining, but my own decades of social activism have taken their toll on me. Let me tell you a story.

A few years back I heard about a rapper named Ice-T who was selling a CD called *"Cop Killer"* celebrating ambushing and murdering police officers. It was being marketed by none other than Time/Warner, the biggest entertainment conglomerate in the world.

Police across the country were outraged. Rightfully so, at least one had been murdered. But Time/Warner was stonewalling because the CD was a cash cow for them, and the media were tiptoeing around it because the rapper was black. I heard Time/Warner had a stockholders meeting scheduled in Beverly Hills. I owned some shares at the time, so I decided to attend.

What I did there was against the advice of my family and colleagues. I asked for the floor. To a hushed room of a thousand average American stockholders, I simply read the full lyrics of *"Cop Killer"* —every vicious, vulgar, instructional word.

> *"I got my 12 gauge sawed off*
> *I got my headlights turned off*
> *I'm about to bust some shots off*
> *I'm about to dust some cops off..."*

It got worse, a lot worse. I won't read the rest of it to you. But trust me, the room was a sea of shocked, frozen, blanched faces. The Time/Warner executives squirmed in their chairs and stared at their shoes. They hated me for that.

Then I delivered another volley of sick lyric brimming with racist filth, where Ice-T fantasizes about sodomizing two 12-year old nieces of Al and Tipper Gore.

"She pushed her butt against my ..."

Well, I won't do to you here what I did to them. Let's just say I left the room in echoing silence. When I read the lyrics to the waiting press corps, one of them said "We can't print that." "I know," I replied, "but Time/Warner's selling it."

Two months later, Time/Warner terminated Ice-T's contract. I'll never be offered another film by Warner's, or get a good review from Time magazine. But disobedience means you must be willing to act, not just talk.

When a mugger sues his elderly victim for defending herself ... jam the switchboard of the district attorney's office.

When your university is pressured to lower standards until 80% of the students graduate with honors choke the halls of the board of regents.

When an 8-year-old boy pecks a girl's cheek on the playground and gets hauled into court for sexual harassment ... march on that school and block its doorways.

When someone you elected is seduced by political power and betrays you ... petition them, oust them, banish them.

When Time magazine's cover portrays millennium nuts as deranged, crazy Christians holding a cross as it did last month ... boycott their magazine and the products it advertises.

So that this nation may long endure, I urge you to follow in the hallowed footsteps of the great disobediences of history that freed exiles, founded religions, defeated tyrants, and yes, in the hands of an aroused rabble in arms and a few great men, by God's grace, built this country.

If Dr. King were here, I think he would agree.

[Charlton Heston's speech at the Harvard Law School Forum, February 16, 1999, is reproduced with permission.]

Typography

This book was set in Times Roman, designed by Stanley Morison specifically for the *Times* of London. The typeface was introduced in the newspaper in 1932. Times Roman had its greatest success in the United States as a book typeface, rather than one used in newspapers.

The book was written and designed using Corel Ventura 8 publishing software. It was printed digitally--using IBM Print-on-Demand technology--by Lightning Source Inc., a subsidiary of Ingram Book Company.

Introduction

American taxpayers spend 2.6 percent of the Gross Domestic Product on maintaining — what we are told — the greatest university system of the whole world. Without any doubt, it is the envy of the rest of the world. No wonder: In proportion, the American higher education system consumes more than twice the GDP that industrialized countries like Germany and Japan spend on higher education, according to *Forbes* magazine (July 24, 2000). Did the taxpayers get their money's worth? They certainly did. But does this huge $ 200 billion a year enterprise operate efficiently? Definitely not.

First of all, it is wasteful. It squanders a lot of resources, not only in the form of money but also in human talent. Secondly, in some parts it is also dishonest, unscrupulous, and self serving.

Do people really benefit from a college education? The knee-jerk reaction of the indoctrinated reader agrees, praising the value of the liberal arts. They are indispensable, one is told, although to what is not clear. Do they form strong, analytical, critical minds? Do they allow the graduate to make good use of the lots of leisure time that is coming, thanks to the efforts of our scientists? Do they inculcate moral values, make model citizens, create a cadre of humanitarians? Do they develop creativity and bring out one's native gifts? That they do is the centuries-old hogwash that is fed to prospective students who don't know any better.

Rather than using undefinable cliches, the contribution of a college education can be clearly expressed in "value added" terms. In one word: money. Bills and coins notwithstanding, money itself is merely an agreed upon representation of "value." Outside of research leading to marketable products, and training students to perform a lifelong service to the community and the nation — a professional service — colleges and universities can offer nothing that a person can not attain on his or her own. Some colleges do neither research nor professional training.

Every time a holder of a B.A. in History has to take a cashier's job at K-Mart, she was cheated by her college. When an entrepreneur can't fill an electrical engineering position that pays $ 85,000 a year, it is the universities that failed him. Every high-school graduate who was not required to take a course in Physics received an education that poorly prepare him or her for the twenty-first century. His teachers, trained in the nation's colleges, messed up his life.

America's greatness and unsurpassed wealth were created by knowledge. Surveyors designed the Erie Canal that opened up the Midwest. Railroads traversing the continent linked the country together. Engineers of the Bureau of Reclamation made California's arid Imperial Valley the garden of the nation, and filled the desert with air-conditioned metropolises from Scottsdale to San Diego. Medical diagnostic, therapeutic and pharmacological advances improved healthcare for all. The country's advance came from the backbreaking work of its citizens and the application of knowledge. The latter was the contribution of the universities of America.

Not all fields contribute equally. For instance, there isn't a single college degree in science or engineering where Physics would not be a fundamental requirement. Yet 82 percent of American college students do not take a single course in Physics. As a result they are unable to grasp even the most fundamental concepts of semiconductors, fiberoptics,

LASIC, CAT scan, MNR scans and other devices of everyday life. Spell out the latter: "nuclear magnetic resonance," basic words from Physics 101 vocabulary; for many college graduates it could as well have been said in Chinese. Mathematics is an even better determinant of the value of a college degree. It should be required for all. Even a person with a B.A. in Social Science should be able to understand statistics. No businessman can function without understanding the concept of compound interest. Colleges in America churn out vast number of graduates who haven't taken a single course in college mathematics. Only 21 percent do. They are the ones with marketable degrees. Many other graduates of America's colleges are fully prepared to cope with the pre-industrial age.

As if the misdirection of a majority of careers were not bad enough, there is a virulent anti-American, Communist insurgency among a segment of the liberal arts faculty at many of our most respected universities. They are engaged in the most monstrous project of social engineering ever committed against a nation from the inside. They attempt to indoctrinate their students to be anti-white, anti-capitalist, anti-Christian; anti-everything that America stands for.

In the following pages the present status of the nation's higher education is reviewed. In order to add substance, it was attempted to support the information with factual data from academic and governmental publications. As Senator Daniel Patrick Moynihan once stated, "everyone is entitled to his own opinion but not his own facts." The facts assembled give a devastating picture of a part of America's colleges and universities, thank God, only a very small part. America's schools are still graduating excellent "knowledge workers," many professors are performing superb research that contributes tremendous value to the nation. The positives overwhelm the negatives. But there are serious problems.

How come this nation is unable to train its own work force? Why does this nation have to import thousands of software engineers from India each year? Why do American colleges train teachers who cannot teach the children mathematics and science? Who is responsible? The higher education system, of course.

These — often critical — observations do not come from an envious and malevolent outsider. The writer possesses a Ph.D. in Engineering from one of the Big Ten schools, and has taught for thirty years at state universities in the Midwest, most of that time serving as department head, supervising the training of about a 1,000 B.S., M.S. and Ph.D.s in engineering.

Andrew L. Simon
Safety Harbor, Florida

1. Why College?

This generation of American university students can enjoy the benefits of having the world's best higher education system available at a very reasonable cost. America trains the best doctors, lawyers, engineers, computer scientists, business administrators, nuclear physicists, polymer chemists, physical therapists, nurses, accountants and economists. There are excellent research laboratories, superbly equipped libraries, and computing facilities that are the envy of the world. American university professors garner the most Nobel Prizes every year.

The United States is a great place to get an education — as long as one goes to the right place to get it. It is, unfortunately, quite easy to get off course, to end up at a college that will prove to be a dead-end place. To learn an economically valuable profession, one has to go to a university. Of the 3,800 plus accredited institutes of higher education, no more than some 300 offer a full plate.

Overall, the economic value of a degree is apparent. According to the U.S. Census Bureau, the average yearly income in 1997 for people with different credentials was:

- Less than 9th grade education - $ 19,291
- High-school graduates - $ 31,215
- Associate degree holders - $ 38,022
- Bachelor degree holders - $ 53,450
- Masters degree holders - $ 61,690
- Professionals (doctors, lawyers, etc.) - $ 85,011

As these figures show, college graduates, on the average, earn more than high school graduates, over 60 percent more. However, this premium is slipping each year. If one factors out doctors, lawyers, engineers, and others whose profession requires state licensing—that prescribes a well defined academic background and several years of supervised professional experience—the remainder of the college graduates would not show up a lot better financially when compared to high-school graduates. More than one in five college graduates earns less than the average high-school graduate. These are the unhappy lot who have taken bachelor degrees in fields deemed worthless in the marketplace. The time and money invested is a drag on the national economy, unless one considers the cost of maintaining America's bloated higher educational establishment a worthy goal in itself.

There are great opportunities ahead of today's college students. In the decade ending in 2006, a 14 percent growth is projected in employment due to economic growth in the United States, according to the U. S. Bureau of Labor Statistics. Most of this growth will happen in fields requiring college degrees. For professionals, doctors, lawyers and highly trained engineers, the expected increase in available positions will be 18 percent. An even greater rate of growth is projected for holders of Bachelor's degrees, 25.4 percent. Close to this rate of growth is projected for holders of two-year Associate degrees, 22.2 percent, (although the total number of job openings for this category is much smaller than those waiting for bachelor's degree holders: 1.6 million versus 7.3 million). Master's degree recipients and those gaining Doctoral degrees are also expected to grow faster than the national average: 15 and 19 percent, respectively. In all, going to college will improve one's chances to get a suitable job, due to the rate of economic growth of America. In comparison, those without college will have relatively fewer employment opportunities.

But university degrees are not needed for about 70 percent of the jobs in the United States. The fastest growing occupations in the beginning of the new century will require no college education, according to labor statisticians. In our growing economy, there will be plenty of jobs in well paying industries. According to the U. S. Bureau of Labor Statistics, in sales and sales-related fields, over 811,000 new positions will open up between 1996 and 2006. There will be a need for over 384,000 new machinists in America in the same period. Demand for new employees as clerical supervisors, maintenance repair technicians, food service and lodging managers, and many other fields will be great. Most of these positions pay considerably better than jobs for those who completed several popular four-year college degree programs.

A young person who does not spend four years taking courses at a college can utilize the time to learn many valuable things, have a multitude of useful experiences, and accomplish many things that prepare him or her for a successful lifetime career. The time saved from college gives a considerable head start over college graduates, not only in getting ahead in a career, but also financially. Many of the relatively unknown, small private colleges charge over $ 20,000 a year nowadays. Adding incidental expenses, the cost of a four-year college degree could easily exceed $ 100,000 pre-tax dollars. If a parent would put this $ 100,000 into a relatively secure investment — rather than into the pocket of an educational establishment—it could easily grow to a half a million dollars in 30 years. That is far more money than the savings the average college educated individual has accumulated at the time of his or her retirement. The savings can also be turned into an investment in a business, boosting the chance for a child's future economic well-being.

To acquire knowledge, going to college is not a necessary requirement. All one needs is a good library nearby and an ardent desire to learn something. Self-educated people have the advantage in that they do not read in order to find the answers approved by half-baked examining boards; they find an individual point of view.

Thomas A. Edison did not have his mind pickled by college teachers. He never went to school. His mother taught him at home. He sought answers to questions without alleged "prior knowledge" of what could or could not be done. As a result, he generated over 1,100 patents. He did it at the time when the director of the U.S. Patent Office suggested that his office be eliminated, on the ground that everything has already been invented. Without Edison's inventions, life would not be like it is today.

The man who started the 250,000 employee company that manufactures electronic products found in practically every American home under names like Panasonic, JVC, Quasar, Technics and countless others, Konosuke Matsushita was forced by poverty at age ten to apprentice himself in a bicycle shop. For several years he worked 80 hours a week. He built one of Japan's largest corporations virtually without the benefit of any education.

For many well-paying positions, college degrees do not appear to be necessary. Each year *Forbes* magazine prepares a list of the largest corporations of the United States, including a short description of their Chief Executive Officers. *Forbes*[1] reported that almost 15.4 percent—58 of the

1   December 28, 1998.

400—of CEOs had no college degrees. The personal net worth of these 58 CEOs amounted to $ 4.8 billion for each, on the average. According to *Forbes,* the $ 4.8 billion was much greater than the average net worth of those Forbes 400 leaders who had degrees from Ivy League colleges. *Those without college degrees accumulated 67 percent more wealth than the Ivy League graduates.*

Indeed, there is no end to the list of successful people who made it without the benefit of a college education. Achievement based on one's talent is not a necessary consequence of university training. In America's history, college was not a prerequisite for success. George Washington, Andrew Jackson, Martin Van Buren, Zachary Taylor, Millard Fillmore, Abraham Lincoln, Andrew Johnson, Grover Cleveland and Harry Truman never attended college. John D. Rockefeller, Henry Ford, Andrew Carnegie, Orville and Wilbur Wright and Ransom Eli Olds did not go to college either. Neither did John Major, former Prime Minister of Britain. Bill Gates was followed by scores of other college dropouts in creating successful corporations. And not only techno- nerds can be mentioned as successes. "Kentucky Colonel" Harland Sanders of fried chicken fame was a seventh grade drop-out. One of America's most successful playwrights, Neil Simon never went to college. Neither did CNN's Larry King. British novelist Len Deighton graduated from art school and worked as an illustrator before he switched careers and started writing his international bestsellers. Radio talk-show host and political commentator Rush Limbaugh never finished college. Ann Landers, whose real name is Eppie Lederer, has only a ninth grade education. Her twin sister, who writes the "Dear Abby" columns, did not go any farther. Eppie's husband, Jules Lederer, founded Budget Rent-a-Car without the benefit of a college education. During the Vietnam War, famous film maker Steven Spielberg wanted to go to college, mainly to avoid the draft. He was rejected by the best schools of cinematography, USC and UCLA. Accepted at Long Beach State, he dropped out as soon as his first film met with success. Another legendary film maker, Stanley Kubrick, maker of *Spartacus, Paths of Glory, Dr. Strangelove, A Clockwork Orange, 2001* and others, did not go to college. "I never learned anything at all in school" was his favorite taunt.

The list goes on. For the really talented, college could get in the way.

There is always a contrasting example. Joy Covey, for instance, 36-year-old chief financial officer of Amazon.com — a company with a 300 % sales growth in 1998 — quit high-school at 16. After earning a high school equivalency degree, she went to Fresno State University and graduated at age 19 with a degree in business administration. After earning the second highest score in the nation on the C.P.A. examination, she joined one of the major accounting firms for a couple of years. She then took a joint degree in law and business at Harvard.

The two owners of Broadcomm, the leading maker of computer networking microchips, Henry Samueli and Henry Nicholas, are similar examples of success through knowledge. In 1985 Samueli was a young electrical engineering professor at UCLA. His first doctoral student was Nicholas. Together they developed an innovative chip and started a business in 1991. By the year 2000 they were among the world's richest people, having a private wealth of over 5 billion each.

Basically, the decision to go or not to go to college should rest almost entirely on economic considerations. Many college degrees have virtually no value on the marketplace.

According to the U. S. Bureau of Labor Statistics, the average monthly salary of a liberal arts graduate in the year 1996 was $ 1,733. In the same year a recipient of a bachelor of science degree in biology made, on the average, $ 1,990 a month. Meanwhile, real estate brokers, on the average, made $ 4,259 a month in a job that, at most, requires two college courses. A legal secretary with good typing skills and some intelligence earned $ 2,258 a month on average, no college required. A well-trained machinist made $ 2,115 a month. A teacher's salary is barely one half the income of an insurance salesman. The teacher must spend four years in college to be certified to teach, while the insurance salesman can learn on the job. So why acquire a degree if it has no economic advantage? The love of learning? Does it really need an auditorium, a lectern, an instructor with a Ph.D. and a dean of students to enforce the college's speech code?

Many people with no college education earn a decent living. The median income — this means that the same number earns more as earn less — of a truck driver in America in 1998 was $ 26,468; the median income of a postal carrier was $ 35,932. These salaries are not very much, but if compared to the median income of a male medical doctor—$ 63,440—they begin to look quite respectable[2]. Imagine how much a physician had to study and how many years it took before he started earning this money, compared to the other two. Overall, the median weekly income of people

2   It must be noted that the mean income for heart doctors in 1997 was $ 284,000 according to the AMA *Physicians Socioeconomic Statistics* of 1999.

with bachelor's degrees was reported to be $ 716 in the year 1996. In the same year 9.3 million workers without college degrees earned $ 700 or more a week. These numbers prove that there are numerous college graduates in America's labor pool with economically worthless degrees.

There is an immense group of well paid blue collar workers between jobs requiring no formal education beyond a high-school diploma and professional careers. They are the people who built America and keep it going. Machinists, tool and die makers, carpenters, plumbers, electricians, printers and computer repair technicians; they all need a considerable amount of training. The class-room study required to obtain a Construction Electrician Diploma at a technical college requires about 73 semester credits—about two and one-half years of academic work, plus years of apprenticeship. There is no academic fluff in these 73 credits; they include courses on the National Electrical Code, electrical theory, courses on wiring, electric motors, controls, electric heating and so on. The rewards are great. A licensed electrician can make over $ 30,000 a year. He can invest about $ 25,000 in an appropriately equipped van, and can start his own business. It sure beats a Bachelor of Arts degree in Social Studies.

Machinists are an even better example. There are 400,000 of them in the United States and their average yearly earnings is $ 55,000. With overtime, they can earn more than $ 100,000. Today's tool-rooms are antiseptically clean, and look like Silicon Valley laboratories with their computer-controlled lathes and drill presses. The $ 40 billion machine tool industry is the heart of America's manufacturing. Opportunities for advancement are limitless; starting on the shop floor, a capable machinist can move up to executive level as superintendent of manufacturing. A well trained machinist can open his own shop with a relatively small investment, and with a bit of luck can build a million-dollar business. Today the average machinist in America is 50 years old, looking forward to retirement. Only 15 thousand youngsters enter the trade yearly and there were 30,000 positions that were unfilled in 1998. Why? Perhaps school guidance counselors still think of the machine tool industry in terms of the bygone Rust Belt.

High school guidance counselors stress college education over vocational training, even though a significant proportion of their charges never make it through high school. In Florida, for instance, over 50 percent of high school students do not graduate in four years. They can't handle the requirements, as low as they are. The majority of the high-school students who could not manage college work would need more attention by high school counselors.

There are perfectly capable students who are inclined to be doers rather than learners. They should be offered more opportunities to learn valuable trades. But there are only about 500 vocational high-schools in the United States. Many of the vocations offered at these schools are obsolete. Students trying to enter vocational careers are often on their own. Guidance books and other information tend to stress college careers. One notable book on the subject of alternative (non-college) education was written by Harlow G. Unger[3] which is full of informative data on the topic. There are scores of addresses of organizations in the book dealing

3   Harlow G. Unger: *"But What If I Don't Want To Go To College?"* New York: Facts On File, Inc, 1998

with apprenticeship programs and similar training for all sorts of fields.

Businesses are clamoring for skilled workers. Vocational education is making a comeback. Business - school partnerships to create practical job training programs are gaining popularity. In 1996, according to the National School-to-Work Office, in one year the number of such partnerships more than doubled to 136,000 nationwide. Businesses offer high school students internships, mentors and on-the-job training. Businessmen, in turn, have the opportunity to observe the students for months before committing themselves with a job offer.

There are hundreds of self-styled "elite" liberal-arts colleges offering their services to a highly selected few "qualified" applicants. Most of the degrees available at these select schools do not prepare their recipients for minimal survival skills in today's society. Learning nineteenth century liberal-arts subjects for the global economy of the twenty-first century's highly technological fields will not be adequate to earn a decent living, without additional years of graduate or professional study.

It is not that graduates with a firm background in classical literature, art history or foreign languages would be entirely unemployable. Generally they have one important thing in common: they probably have excellent communication skills. They are trained in analyzing concepts, and communicating ideas. The better ones are also highly creative. In these abilities liberal arts graduates are very much like those people who are eagerly sought by high technology companies. The creative people in the twenty-first century are not likely to climb up scaffolds painting scenes on church ceilings. They interact with their peers, brainstorm, and think up newer and newer schemes in Internet commerce, computer technology, software design and telecommunications. Only a tiny segment of these high-tech people are esoteric hardware designers or software gurus; the rest are from all walks of life with a single thing in common — superior intellect. They are quick-witted, intellectually flexible, resourceful, creative, and ready to adapt to new situations. The high-tech industry of today is the most non-hierarchic, egalitarian, fast-moving, productive community the world has ever seen. To be a part of such creative groups is a great deal of fun, contrary to the grossly uninformed and envious opinions of English professors who assert that technology is boring. How one gets into this business is irrelevant. The demand for talent is so great in places like Silicon Valley that anyone with a sound educational background has a chance to get in. Once one is inside, the sky is the limit.

Alas, one has less and less chance in America to acquire a "fine liberal-arts education." Aristotle and Shakespeare are increasingly replaced in college curricula by vapid third world authors to give the students the rather dubious "benefit" of non-European viewpoints on the world. Western culture may be emulated throughout the world but in America's "elite" liberal-arts colleges, voodoo and queer theory are taking over.

A lot of "liberal arts" knowledge is readily available without going to college. Take foreign languages, for instance. Most small liberal arts colleges offer majors in foreign languages. The languages offered are rarely other than German, French and Spanish. But it is hard to find native college graduates in America who actually can speak a foreign language that he or she learned in college. It is a pity, as the demand of industry for managerial level employees who speak foreign languages is growing rapidly. The U. S. Department of Education reported that there are over 30 federal agencies that regularly recruit people to fill some 34,000 positions that require foreign language proficiency. They can wait a long time to find American college-educated speakers of critical languages. Altogether only about one percent of American students study either Russian, Chinese or Japanese according to the American Council on the Teaching of Foreign Languages. At the same time, 22 percent of students study French in American schools. Aside from paying the salaries of French teachers, there isn't much benefit from their efforts.

The Federal Government has spent billions of dollars to teach American diplomats and CIA officers every conceivable foreign language from Swahili to Urdu. For a couple of hundred dollars anybody can purchase the tapes developed at the Foreign Language Institute of the State Department and learn any language, without the assistance of a college instructor. All one has to do is call Audio-Forum (203 453-9794) for the textbook and tapes for any of the over one hundred languages offered.

Many liberal arts students major in English. Europeans view this with amusement. Spending four years in college studying one's own native language appears strange to them. But be it as it may, one could not wish for a better teacher of the roots of the English language than having access to the *Etymological Dictionary* created by Father Eugene J. Cotter of Seton Hall University. This Internet website all but eliminates the need for printed dictionaries to search Latin and Greek words appearing in classical English texts. The address is

http://www.ablemedia.com/ctcweb/show-case/roots.html

In Father Cotter's words: " you don't even need a teacher."

The real forte of small liberal arts colleges is the teaching of Western literature. It is also available for a few hundred dollars on audio or video cassettes taught by the country's most eminent professors in 80 lectures published by The Teaching Company. The same company offers a cross-cultural exploration of 2,500 years of political theory from the ancient Greeks to Hitler, in a 16-lecture video and/or audio course. Other topics, like the history of religions, are also available on their website:

http://www.teachco.com/

One doesn't need to live near a library anymore to have access to the great books. Just check out the *Great Books Online* at

http://www.bartleby.com/

There are more books available on the Internet for anyone with a computer and a modem than in the libraries of most small colleges. As early as in 1971, Michael Hart at the Materials Research Laboratory of the University of Illinois initiated a project with a goal to make available 10,000 books in E-text form by 2001 on the *Project Gutenberg Electronic Library.* Thanks to the many volunteers, it appears to be well ahead of schedule. The Gutenberg website is found at

http://promo.net/pg/list.html#list

Another great collection of books is *The Internet Public Library* at

http://www.ipl.org/reading/books

It alone has over 7,000 titles.

An immense worldwide collection of Internet websites is the *WWW Virtual Library for the History of Science, Technology & Medicine:*

http://www.asap.unimelb.edu.au/hstm/hstm_alp.htm

Want to learn history? The *Historical Text Archive* on the Internet is an tremendous collection of history books:

http://www.geocities.com/Athens/Forum/9061/index.html

The *World Wide Web Virtual Library* is another great site with links to all over the world

http://history.cc.ukans.edu/history/www_history_main.html

As they say in Britain of someone who was a history student at Oxford: "He read history at Oxford." As can be seen from these Internet addresses, one can read at home, all that's needed is a computer. Learning opportunities outside the ivy-covered walls of academia are endless, thanks to the Internet.

One of the most significant reasons that literally force the most capable and intelligent of our youth into college comes from an entirely unacademic source. It has to do with the Supreme Court's decision in 1971, the lawsuit known as Griggs vs. Duke Power Company, which effectively outlawed the use of IQ tests in hiring. As a result, if a company owner is in need of a few good men and women, he can not select them directly on the basis of their relative intelligence as determined by a national IQ test. Hence the next best thing is to require that the applicants have a college degree. In a sense, it is an artificial gimmick to force young men and women into college who would not consider it otherwise. It is great for the education establishment of America. It takes off millions of young people from the unemployment rolls over a period of four years. It keeps huge numbers of professors and support personnel in well paid and secure jobs, whose taxes contribute to the government coffers. Many of these professors couldn't find a job on the marketplace outside of academia. This way they can justify their existence.

There are few occupations in America today that do not require some kind of license or certificate by the state. Many of these, like licensing of doctors, have obvious reasons. But in general, "credentialing" quite often serves the profession itself by reducing the number who are allowed to perform the work. Mediaeval guilds did the same thing. They artificially maintained a source of cheap labor by controlling the number of their apprentices and maximizing the years they had to serve. Modern guilds conspire against the public to keep their numbers small, hence keeping their prices high. In today's world it is the educators who insist that their services be required in every instance a young person wants to better his or her chances to a better life, even if there is convincing evidence that having a prescribed diploma to do something does not, in fact, improve one's performance. As a 1969 Ford Foundation report said: "We have become a credential society in which one's educational level is more important than what he can do." Cutting back the course offerings at universities would help. As long as students strain to qualify for the myriads of pseudo-professions, they need the hundreds of courses – gladly offered by America's 550,000 professors – leading through various paths to jobs. Alas, our schools are moving in the opposite direction. The number of courses offered is growing, rather than shrinking.

The states' and the guilds' power to control access to professions is enforced through licensing boards and tests such
as the bar examination. Often there are no appeals to high-
handed bureaucratic inequities.

There are few uncredentialed industries left. Professional
sports and the arts are two exceptions. In these highly competitive occupations, performance is judged by the score-
board or the audience. No one cares how they did on the
Scholastic Aptitude Test. But if an Olympic champion
wants to teach a sport or a successful artist wants to teach
art, only the diploma matters. One's skill as a performer –
or, for that matter, a teacher – is irrelevant.[4] Other endeavors
not requiring a state license are professional writing and the
movie industry. Also, lest we forget: politics and organized
crime.

The question of why young people go to college was recently answered on a survey conducted by the American
Council on Education with the cooperation of the University of California at Los Angeles. In the fall of 1997 they
surveyed 252,082 freshmen entering 464 two-year and
four-year institutions. The results were statistically adjusted to represent the approximately 1.61 million first-
time, full-time freshmen of America. The final report of this
research study was first published by *The Chronicle of
Higher Education*[5]. Since then it was widely quoted in the

4   David Hapgood: *Diplomaism;* Buffalo:
     Prometheus, 1971.

5   *The Chronicle of Higher Education,* Aug. 27,
     1999.

news media. The answers are interesting because they represent the views of those students who are called the millennial generation, who were born in the early 1980s, who will live their productive life in the beginning of the third millennium. Here are some of the most important results:

Freshmen said that their main reasons to go to college were

- to be able to get a better job (74.6 %)
- to learn more about things that interest them (74.3 %)
- to be able to make more money (73.0 %)

The idealistic dreams of bettering the world, helping others, love of learning and so on have taken the back seat compared to the pragmatic and practical world-view of today. How they selected their college is also revealing. Their most popular answers to such questions were:

- school has a very good academic reputation (53.9 %)
- graduates get good jobs (50.3 %)
- financial assistance offered by the school (33.8 %)

All of these indicate a goal-oriented, pragmatic and down-to-earth approach to life by today's freshmen.

In questions regarding non-economic issues the students' answers showed that they generally disregarded social activities at the college. Today's students are hard-nosed about academic progress and economic considerations. And they expect to be successful. Two thirds expect to get their bachelor's degree — slightly more women than men—and they expect to get a job while in college to help with finances (40.3 percent). They have little inclination to join a fraternity, sorority or a club (only 15.8 percent showed interest) and do not plan to participate in student protests and demonstrations (only 4.4 percent do). In 1969, according to Gallup polls, 28 percent of students participated in student demonstrations. Building takeovers and violent demonstrations were the rule in the late sixties. This dropped to 19 percent by 1976. In 1998 only two sit-ins occurred, at Georgetown and Duke Universities. These involved only a tiny minority, 27 and 20 individuals, respectively. Today's students are definitely more civilized than those of the 1960s. Then again, there is no draft to dodge.

Another interesting statistical datum is that 81.5 percent attended religious activities in the past year and 73.1 percent participated in volunteer work, but only 13.7 percent discussed politics. To become an authority in their field was the aim of 62.8 percent, but being very well off financially topped that at 74.9 percent. 72.8 percent planned to raise a family.

Today's college students want knowledge that leads to economic well-being. They want the degrees required for well paid jobs, and these are degrees that lead to graduate and professional schools, or to bachelor degrees in business management, accounting, various engineering disciplines, computer science, physics, mathematics and statistics, and other fields sought by industry and commerce.

The proportion of students entering college in the United States is the highest in the world. The U.S. also has the highest dropout rates of all industrialized countries, 37 percent. Obviously, over one in three college students in America gets disenchanted with his or her educational choice and drops out.

Interestingly, a college degree doesn't necessarily bring happiness. 1998 George Mason University conducted a survey of 400 college graduates and found that nearly half wished they had selected a field in science and technology, rather than their own. But those in the high-tech fields were not much happier; 40 percent stated they would rather be in another field, such as education.

The simple truth about the true value of going to college was spelled out by America's greatest management "guru," Peter Drucker:

"The best investment around, by far, is professional school. Whether it is engineering school, medical school, law school or library school, business school or architecture school, graduation from one of them increases a person's lifetime earning power by a substantial multiple of the <u>investment</u>, that is, of the cost of his or her education. Not all professional schools produce the same economic benefits, of course. But even the ones of the least "yield" (probably schools of education, social work and library science) endow their graduates with the potential of earning well above the median American income." [6]

6   Peter F. Drucker: *The Frontiers of Management,*
     New York: Plume/Penguin Group, 1999.

2. Past and Present

American colleges and universities at the advent of the twenty-first century have developed from a curious mixture of European and typically American traditions. To understand the current difficulties and problems of the nation's higher education one must understand its history. Here is a short review:

Mediaeval universities, following the practice started by Oxford in England, the Sorbonne in France and Bologna in Italy, came about as compacts between teachers and students. The topics taught were mainly theology and philosophy. The latter included subjects like algebra, astronomy and all other sciences of the day. Most graduates became polymaths, meaning that they knew just about everything worth knowing. Teaching language and virtually all books were Latin. Students came from all over civilized Europe. The concept of nationalism was not born yet. Outside influences from secular or religious powers were negligible. Teaching and learning were strictly a matter between students and teachers.

In the age of Reformation things changed. Protestants sent their future preachers to the universities of Wittenberg, Leiden, Heidelberg and others. Jesuits organized universities to defend the Catholic faith. In those days, outside of religious matters, societal concerns did not influence higher education.

Even in the middle of the eighteenth century, university teaching was directed toward the students as individuals. The founder of modern economic thought, Adam Smith, a professor at Glasgow University, was paid for his services

directly by his students. Smith liked the system. He said:
Teacher's diligence "is likely to be proportioned to the motive which he has for exerting it."

In the age of Enlightenment secular education came to the forefront. Individual efforts to teach and learn were superseded by the needs of society. In Europe the much maligned Habsburg Monarchy was the leader in this movement. In 1777 Empress Maria Theresa[1] issued a law proclaiming strict government control of all levels of education. She set up a commission to introduce rationalism into teaching, and to draw up a government required curriculum in mathematics, physics, natural sciences, writing and physical education. It was enforced and supervised by powerful government officials. The educational concepts espoused came from the ideas of the French Enlightenment. It is remarkable that this was decreed by the mother of Marie Antoinette, who allegedly urged hungry peasants to eat cake when they didn't have bread. (Historians say that it wasn't quite so, but it sounded good enough for those bent on revolution.)

Practical considerations concerning societal needs on Habsburg lands precipitated decisive governmental actions. For the first time in history, higher education was deployed

1   Istvan Meszaros: *The Thousand Year History of Schools in Hungary*, Budapest: Nat'l Textbook Publ., 1999.

to apply the institutions' knowledge for the benefits of society. If the existing ones were inadequate for the work at hand, new universities were created. For instance, as mines got deeper, extraction of coal and ores became more difficult and expensive. To remedy the problem, Maria Theresa decreed on September 17, 1763 that a college of mining and smelting is to be established at the mines of Selmec, in Northern Hungary,[2] to train mining and metallurgical engineers for all her lands. Teaching at the new school commenced that fall. Mineralogy and Metallurgy was taught by Vilmos Jaquin. His yearly salary was set at 2,000 golden thalers, a princely sum at the time. It was paid by the government, not by students, as had been the case with Adam Smith only a few years earlier. By 1770 additional faculty was hired, a library was started, geology and mineralogy collections were purchased and laboratories were built. Initial enrollment was 140 students, half of whom received royal stipends. A high school diploma, two years of practical experience in mining and royal permission were the admission requirements. A unique feature of the curriculum was the incorporation of field and laboratory work to provide practical training along with a scientific one. Research at the college led to new mining techniques, de-watering pumps, the lead-electrolyte battery, an early form of the modern mining machine, and the smelting technique called amalgamation. The College of Mining at Selmec Mine attracted students from all over Europe.

During the French Revolution, in 1794, barely a year after the execution of Queen Marie-Antoinette, France's Na-

2   Banska Stiavnica, now Slovakia, in 1920 the
     university was relocated to Sopron, Hungary.

tional Convention established the *École Polytechnique* in Paris. The country needed roads and bridges and to build these, first it needed engineers. In an address to the Convention, Assemblyman Antoine Fourcroy, famed neuro- physiologist and co-discoverer of the element Iridium, recommended that the College of Mining of Selmec be adopted as a pattern for France's new engineering school. The school evolved into one of France's elite group of *grandes écoles*, which admit, even today, only the best of the very best students of the country. Like West Point, graduates also qualify for an officer's commission in the French army.

Habsburg Emperor Joseph II, son of Maria Theresa, was another pragmatic monarch. He addressed societal problems with academic solutions. In his case, the issue was the reclamation of the great plain that is now the eastern half of Hungary. It was largely a malaria-ridden swamp that was flooded every year so as to be almost uninhabitable. In 1782, to control the floods and drain the swamps, Joseph II established the *Institutum Geometrico et Hidrotechnicum*. This Institute of Surveying and Hydrotechnics was made a component of the nationalized University of Science in Budapest, a college originally established in 1635 by the Jesuits. Thus the world's first university-level engineering school was created. It trained engineers to map the country and design flood-control measures. The institute produced thousands of hydraulic engineers, whose work resulted in the completion of the biggest public works project in 19th century Europe, protecting over 8,000 square miles of fertile farmland from floods, an area about the size of Massachusetts.

Although initiated by the Habsburg Monarchs, it took Prussian organization skills to generalize the concept of the modern university as the servant of society at large. The tradition that universities were not only places of learning but also places of industrial and economic innovation started in the early years of the nineteenth century. Wilhelm von Humboldt at the University of Berlin introduced the concept of "research university." Humboldt declared: "The teacher no longer serves the purposes of the student. Instead they both serve learning itself." This was the model that became the guiding light for the evolution of the modern university.

The German model was adopted throughout Europe and was soon imported into the United States, but by that time the system of colleges in America was firmly established. According to some reports, there were as many as 800 colleges in America before the Civil War. Hence the concept of research university was overlaid on this existing system of small, local, humanities-oriented network of colleges. The latter, numbering over 180 in America after the Civil War, were fractioned by their religious, racial and ethnic orientations. Most were small and financially shaky. Their curriculum, regimented and authoritarian, was mired in the past. They claimed to form strong, analytical, critical minds, inculcate moral values, train model citizens, create humanitarians, and develop their students' creativity. Whether their claims were justified is not the issue here. Their declared aims never really mixed well with the new university model: serving society, the nation.

A major study of American higher education by Jencks and Riesman explains:

"During the seventeenth, eighteenth, and early nineteenth centuries, American colleges were conceived and operated as pillars of the locally established church, political order, and social conventions. These local arrangements were relatively stable, widely accepted as legitimate, and comparatively well integrated with one another. Yet while the pre-Jacksonian college was almost always a pillar of the establishment, it was by no means a very important pillar. An American "college" was in some respects more like today's secondary schools than today's universities. It did not employ a faculty of scholars. Indeed, only one or two pre-Jackson- ian college teachers exercised any significant influence on the intellectual currents of their time. An always upright and usually erudite clergyman served as president. He then hired a few other men (usually young bachelors and often themselves aspiring clergymen) to assist in the teaching. There were only a few professorships in specialized subjects. In most cases everyone taught almost everything, usually at a fairly elementary level.

"Nor did these American colleges have much impact on the character of the rising generation. Only a minority of those who controlled the established institutions of pre-Jacksonian America sent their children to college, and an even smaller minority had itself been to a college. Even those who attended seldom seem to have regarded the experience as decisive for their later development, at least judging by the relative scarcity of references to colleges in the literature of the time. Unlike leading continental universities, American colleges offered little professional training in fields like medicine, law, or theology. The liberal-arts courses were probably in closer touch with the Enlightenment than their nineteenth-century successors would be with the spirit of their time, but they seldom seem to have played a major role in shaping the minds of America's leading thinkers.

"With the construction of the railroads, the closing of the American frontier, and the rise of industrialization a new era started. Opportunities became greater, the social stratification has changed. The new system was increasingly meritocratic. It tried to divide people according to competence, interest, and achievement rather than according to origin... While there was still plenty of exceptions to the general meritocratic rule, and plenty of reasons for ambivalence about its increasing acceptance, an inevitable feature of highly organized societies was a very specialized division of labor.

"The partial triumph of meritocracy brings with it what we will call the national upper-middle class style: cosmopolitan, moderate, universalistic, somewhat legalistic, concerned with equity and fair play, aspiring to neutrality between regions, religions, and ethnic groups. Not everyone who has money, power, or visibility in America subscribes to this set of ideals even in theory, much less in practice... Nonetheless, we would argue that the ethic we are describing, like the institutions which encourage it, is growing stronger rather than weaker.

"These changes in the character of American society have inevitably been accompanied by changes of education. The most basic of these changes has been the rise of the university. This has had many consequences. College instructors have become less and less preoccupied with educating young people, more and more preoccupied with educating one another by doing scholarly research which advances their discipline. Undergraduate education has become less and less a terminal enterprise, more and more a preparation for graduate school. The result is that higher education has ceased to be a marginal, backward-looking enterprise shunned by the bulk of the citizenry. Today it is a major growth industry, consuming about 2.0 per cent of GNP [written in 1968, in 2000 it is closer to 2.6 %], directly touching the lives of perhaps 4 per cent of the population, and exercising an indirect effect on the whole of society.

"The rise of the university has been gradual rather than sudden. The first Ph.D. was awarded in 1861 by Yale. Cornell opened in 1868 with Andrew White as President. Charles Eliot was inaugurated as President of Harvard in 1869. Yet it was not until the 1880s that anything like a modern university really took shape in America. Perhaps the most important breakthroughs were the founding of Johns Hopkins and Clark as primarily graduate universities. Eliot's success in instituting the elective system at Harvard was also important, both in its own right and because it facilitated the assemblage of a more scholarly and specialized faculty. The 1890s saw further progress, with the founding of Chicago, the reform of Columbia, and the tentative acceptance of graduate work as an important activity in the leading state universities. This was also the period when national learned societies and journals were founded and when knowledge was broken up into its present departmental categories ("physics," "biology," "history," "philosophy," and so forth), with the department emerging as the basic unit of academic administration. Medicine and law also became serious subjects of graduate study at this time, with Johns Hopkins leading the way in medicine and Harvard in law. By World War I two dozen major universities had emerged, and while the number has grown slightly since then, the changes have been slow." [3]

While most colleges and universities in the United States were largely based in the pre-Jacksonian idea of liberal arts schools, catering mainly to the cultural improvement of their students, America's federal government has carried the concept of "universities for the public good" to even greater heights than did European countries. The Morrill Act in 1862 gave the states federal lands on which to establish colleges offering programs in agriculture, engineering and home economics as well as traditional academic subjects and military training. The Hatch Act in 1887 expanded the program with funds for research. These legislative steps gave the United States its land grant universities that are the envy of the civilized world today.

The first American technical school was West Point, founded in 1802 to train army officers who were also capable of building 'civilian' engineering works like bridges and dams. Decades later, in 1824, Rensselaer was founded as a civilian technical school in Troy, New York, and soon it became the center of applied science in the country. Applied

3   Christopher Jencks and David Riesman: *The Academic Revolution*; Doubleday, 1968.

science made inroads on established institutions only in the 1840s. By the time of the Civil War there were about a dozen colleges in the U.S. where future bridge builders, railroad designers, and in some cases experimental farmers were trained. In most cases these new fields were attached to established liberal arts colleges, much to the disdain and chagrin of the faculties of the latter. The liberal arts faculties made it no secret that they considered their applied science colleagues academically inferior. At Yale the scientific students were even segregated from their classmates in chapel. The feelings, however, were mutual. The scientists considered the liberal arts curriculum as uninteresting, impractical, undemanding, and effete.[4] This mutual animosity has not subsided during the past 150 years.

A noted critic of the education establishment, former Glassboro State College professor Richard Mitchell put it well:

"People who make their livings in "soft" sciences and the arts are not entirely at ease in the company of chemists and physicists and other "hard" scientists. In such company, the psychologists and sociologists and the professors of English feel like touch-football enthusiasts who have wandered by mistake into the locker room of the Pittsburgh Steelers. Only true philosophers, not professors of philosophy, are entirely immune to the nasty suspicion that rises in the heart of the "humanist" when he hears about recombinant DNA or quarks. ... This is a modern condition, and quite unlike that of older times, in which the fledgling "hard" scientists were held in contempt by those who did their work entirely in the mind without the help of apparatus'

4   See Jenks, op cit., p. 224.

proper only to artisans. It seems only fair; it's the alchemists' revenge." [5]

Unfortunately, the idea of colleges doing all things for all people was spread far too wide. In our day, every university worth its salt claims in its "mission statement" that its goal is "teaching, research and public service." Even though most mission statements include lofty words about "excellence in teaching", it has gone so far that it is not hard to find an institution where undergraduate teaching serves as nothing more than a cash cow to support the faculty's research activities. This fact is not spotlighted in the mission statement.

Since the nineteenth century, students graduating from secondary schools in most European countries have had to pass a very rigorous state examination. Those who pass this exam are virtually guaranteed admission to universities. This system has worked just fine for quite a while. In France, for example, in the beginning of the twentieth century fewer than 10,000 graduated with the required qualifications each year. But today, the secondary schools produce about a half a million graduates who expect their rightful place to be waiting for them at a university each year. In 1980 there were one million students enrolled in French universities. In 1996 their number exceeded two million. France's top universities, the *grandes écoles,* are extremely selective. The rest of the universities are doing the best they can with the mob. They are swamped, and student riots are

5   Richard Mitchell: *The Graves of Academe,*
      Boston: Little, Brown, 1981.

not infrequent. Forty percent of these students fail to graduate.

The situation in Germany is about the same as in France. While only a limited number of carefully selected students are allowed into professional schools like law, engineering and medicine, others are jammed into overcrowded universities. The number of qualified secondary school graduates has tripled since 1970 and the universities haven't kept up with the growth. In Germany, the problem is somewhat relieved by the traditionally excellent industry-oriented apprenticeship program, which trains much needed technical specialists. In addition, Germany initiated technical institutes somewhat similar to America's two-year technical colleges. In spite of these advances, the German system of higher education is far from being healthy.

In democratic countries governments do not have the will to adopt strict admission policies that discriminate on the basis of ability. Everywhere in the world the middle class yearns for the upward mobility ostensibly secured by a university degree for their children. This puts pressure on society to open up the gates and increase the capacity of universities to put through an ever-increasing number of students. While in the past traditionally twelve percent of the population was sufficient to fill the required professional and civil service positions that needed advanced degrees, today the proportion of college graduates edges up to 30 percent. Critics say that more is worse.

In comparing European systems of higher education to that of America, one must bear in mind W. Arthur Lewis' observation:

"The United States is the only country in the world which thinks that the purpose of going to college is to be educated. Everywhere else one goes to high-school to be educated, but goes to college to be trained for one's life work." [6]

In the United States, according to the 1990 Census, 20.3 percent of the population holds college degrees, bachelor's, master's and doctoral degrees combined. An additional 6.2 percent earned two-year associate degrees. For 30 percent of the population the highest academic level attained was the high school diploma.[7] It follows that 43.5 percent of the U.S. population is left behind.

At public universities, particularly in states where open admission for all state residents is prescribed by law, many entering students lack the prerequisites for college work. This forces these public universities to operate vast remedial programs, teaching what really amounts to high school English and mathematics courses for thousands of students. Fully 78 percent of American universities are forced to offer remedial work to incoming students. This often adds an entire additional year to the student's program. Noticeably, students who graduated from private schools, many times those from Catholic high-schools, are very often fully qualified to start their college programs. Public school students, on the other hand, may require several remedial courses before they are ready for their academic work. This is not an appropriate place to flatly condemn America's public education. It will suffice to say that it is inferior compared to private schools or high schools of foreign countries. Among

6   David Hapgood: *Diplomaism*, Buffalo:
     Prometheus, 1971, p. 38.

7   *The Chronicle of Higher Education*, Aug.
     27,1999.

the world's industrialized countries, the high school students' performance in United States ranks twenty-eighth in mathematics and seventeenth in science. It is not likely to change.

Drastic change is not forthcoming in elementary and secondary education, even though the federal government has some 800 education-related programs administered by about 37 different agencies. Federal funds represent only seven percent of school spending in the United States, some 15 billion dollars a year. After all, education is supposed to be a local matter in America. But the federal money is a carrot. The stick is the activist political agenda of the federal government. It legislates elevators for the handicapped, services for the bilingual child, sport teams for girls and a lot of other programs that Washington bureaucrats love to micro-manage. But whether the teachers are certified to teach their subject matter—or even know it—is of no concern to Washington. Neither is the curriculum taught at our nation's schools. These aspects are regulated by the individual states.

Quality education is important to the economic well being of a country. It is a matter of international competition in which the USA is not doing well at all. In fact, it is falling behind other countries at a rapid pace. In 1990 the average number of years that a five-year-old American was expected to attend high school (and college) was the world's highest, 16.3. In 1996 this has even grown a bit, to 16.8. But meanwhile, eleven other countries, including Canada, Spain and Finland, surpassed that number. To add insult to injury, in the United States a smaller percentage of the national income is devoted to teacher salaries than in other countries.

Discussing the quality of high school education in America today, it is worthwhile to review the admission requirements for girls at Massachusetts' Wellesley College in 1867:

- Be at least 16 years of age and pass examinations in:
- Ancient and modern geography,
- Arithmetics,
- Algebra through involution, evolution and quadratic equations and geometry,
- Latin grammar and four books of Caesar, four books of Virgil and four orations of Cicero and equal amounts of reading of other Latin authors,
- Prepare for examinations in French and German.

When the University of Texas first opened in 1883, students under 18 were required to write a composition on Scott's *Ivanhoe,* Dickens' *Bleak House,* Burns's *Cotter's Saturday Night,* or Goldsmith's *Deserted Village*, but which one they were not told until they sat down at their desk. (People 18 or over could enter without formal tests.) This was before the credit system was invented and the Scholastic Aptitude Test was introduced.

In the developed world — among the 29 member countries of the Organization for Economic Cooperation and Development (OECD) — about 20 percent of the youngsters pursues higher education. They do it mostly at the expense of the taxpayers. The average proportion of the 18 to 21 age bracket in higher education has grown from 14.4 percent in 1985 to 22.4 % in 1995. It must be noted that the tax burden of maintaining public higher education falls mainly on lower income people who make comparatively little use of the universities; the diplomas go to higher income people who pay less than their share of the cost.[8]

There are two ways economists view this phenomenon. One point of view is that college education is a sieve that select the best and the brightest for future employment, rather than providing them with the skills needed for society. Doubtlessly, this is a mighty expensive way of sorting people. Other economists consider college education as building "human capital," which benefits society by making individuals more productive. Even those who do not complete their education get some benefit from their experiences. On the other hand, the larger the proportion of the population that benefits from higher education, the less a college degree will be an indicator of merit.

Not only the numbers but the expenses have grown. Governmental expenditures for higher education in most industrially developed countries account for 1.6 percent of the Gross National Product, in contrast to the U.S. figure of 2.6 percent. By far the largest share of this is met by the taxpayers. Some European countries, just like the United States, are attempting to shift the cost of higher education from the taxpayers to the students who directly benefit from it. Starting with a free system, Britain has recently required its university students to pay a tuition of 1,000 pounds a year, amounting to about $ 1,600 dollars. In 1998, 55 percent of America's college students paid a tuition of a little over $4,000 a year, so our British cousins have a long way to go. In France and Germany, higher education is still practically free. Their systems, already described, are creaking under the load.

8   Hapgood; op. cit.

Throughout the world, universities encounter a major problem: an ever growing number of young people clamor for education but at the same time the academics are clinging to Herr Humboldt's concept of career advancement through research. To overcome the problem, several countries, including America, introduced schemes to provide advanced education without the concomitant "research and public service" label.

The three-layered system introduced in California some thirty years ago is an excellent example. At the top of the system is the nine-campus University of California, containing world-class schools like the U. C. at Berkeley and UCLA. They skim off the top 12 percent or so of the state's best scholars, about 160,000 of them at the last count. In 1998 about 43,000 freshmen enrolled in the system. Under a new rule that will take effect in 2001, the top 4 percent of California's public high-school graduates will be automatically guaranteed a place at the U.C. System.

Under this layer of elite state schools is the multi-campus California State University system with about 340,000 students. The greatness of this setup is that it encourages the individual institutions to specialize. While the U.C. maintains world-class but expensive research universities, the C.S.U. puts a lot less emphasis on research, and provides a cheaper education.

At the bottom layer is the system of community colleges — some 100 of them throughout California — where about 1.4 million students are enrolled. Similar systems exist today in most states.

Community colleges, ridiculed in Europe, are the crown-jewels of America's post-secondary education. At a remarkably low cost, they provide everything from remedial education to preparatory courses toward four-year curricula, including such professional programs as business administration and engineering. And they also offer useful education toward careers from dental hygiene to aircraft mechanics and computer repair.

The problem with this three-tiered model is what is referred to in the ed-biz as "mission creep." Two-year colleges try to position themselves to offer four-year degrees, at least in one or two politically well selected academic fields of study. Snagging the cooperation of a major local industry or a nearby, full-fledged state university is often helpful in this process. Usually, the plan starts out with some narrowly identified bachelor's degree in which a major local industrial firm expresses interest. For the firm it is a cheap way of tentatively selecting and training future employees. The best of the program's graduates will be hired — with the added benefit that they are already familiar with the company's operation through some cooperative internship program which is woven into the curriculum. A bachelor's degree-granting institution offers its assistance in terms of actually granting the degree. The degree-granting institution will produce more degrees without the need for increased facilities on campus. The courses are offered at the community college campus, using cheap part-time instructors. But soon the "need" to hire full-time instructional staff is shown, the need for laboratories is demonstrated (often first using obsolete equipment donated by industry). In a few years the community college asks to be upgraded to four-year status, as "in fact" it already is. In the rush of moving upward, the basic mission of the community college is forgotten.

An extreme example for mission creep is the program the Saint Petersburg Junior College embarked upon in 1999. It linked up with eight Florida institutions, ranging from tiny

St. Leo to major state universities, to offer 22 bachelor's and six master's degrees in a variety of academic fields from engineering to hospitality management. A Doctor of Pharmacy degree was added in the year 2000. It is planned as a three-year, part-time program involving Saturday lectures. Students study from video tapes and through the Internet. [9]

"Mission creep" appears at bachelor-level institutions also. They prepare proposals to extend their offerings into graduate fields by offering master's degrees in this or that. Often this is connected to some local industrial concern which would benefit by offering their employees the possibility of working toward a master's degree part-time, often with a company subsidy. This is a common hiring ploy used in industry, a desirable employment benefit. These schemes then call for new laboratories and extended other facilities that cost a lot of money for no apparent benefit for a large segment of the undergraduates. Faculty members seek opportunities for doing research that leads to professional publications and perhaps better positions elsewhere. Quite often it is done in cooperation with a local firm which, in turn, benefits by having faculty members as high-powered consultants at hand for low, part-time wages. Master's degrees done part-time, after work – without the benefit of a fully staffed comprehensive university at hand with its support departments, library and so on – are only faint ghosts of the real stuff.

9   Finally, in May of 2001, the "junior" was officially removed from SPJR's name.

The "mission creep" extends all the way to doctoral level institutions. Unsatisfied with what they have, and seeking greater glories, they try to position themselves as research universities. Unfortunately, progress like this invariably leads to relatively inferior performance compared to already established research universities.

Collegiality among individual faculty members led to the common academic presumption that everybody is equal. This may be so in the eyes of God. But to say that a professor with an Ed.D. specializing in children's literature is equal to a colleague who has a Ph.D. in astrophysics is a rather eccentric idea. Universities must try to pay their instructors a wage that is roughly comparable to earnings available in industry. A physician teaching at a medical school will demand a salary that is somewhat similar to an income in clinical practice. But such distinctions are generally lost on an academic. The dogma has evolved that if knowledge of the various academic specialties are of equal value, then the compensation should also be the same. To point out value differences from the marketplace of real life is considered in academia to be a rude and absurd suggestion.

The lack of differentiation between subjects offered and the relative economic value of various degrees confuses the consumers. Smaller colleges, like so many stores offering knowledge rather than general merchandise, set up programs that are relatively cheap to offer. In every state there are dozens of four-year colleges within driving distance to their prospective student body offering a variety of enticing academic programs. The admissions officers usually do not point out the relative value of their offerings in terms of the real world. They rather stress the immense intellectual benefit of learning about this and that, be it Egyptian hieroglyphics or Japanese origamy. All this was quite fine when attending a college was a part of indolent life of the ultra-rich, not anymore.

The bachelor's degrees offered by many small liberal-arts colleges will take four years out of their students' lives. The students will mature in this period, and be more able to function as adults in society. They learn some communications skills so that they can write a letter of application for a job. They get a smattering of knowledge about the world they live in. In and out of class they discuss grand policy questions related to society at large, topics that they are highly unlikely to be asked to make decisions about in their later lives, but this background gives them a sense of superiority over their brethren. However, while in school, their tuition enables the college to operate and keep the professors off the welfare rolls. This scheme does wonders for the nation's unemployment statistics.

Prospective students increasingly realize that the training they receive in small cosy colleges is of less practical value than degrees from larger, usually state-supported schools. According to a report by the U.S. Department of Education, in the mid-1960's liberal arts colleges attracted one out of two of all students; while now they enroll fewer than one in five[10].

In the following chapter, the number of doctoral degrees produced at the universities of America will be shown. These Ph.D. degrees' fields or specialties range from Com-

10   Martin Van Der Werf: The Struggle to Define a
       Niche for a Liberal-Arts Institution, *The Chronicle
       of Higher Education*, Dec. 17, 1999.

puter Engineering to Social History. In fact, the number of degrees produced in the hard sciences is fewer and fewer, and that in the humanities is on an increase. The condition is reached that most graduates of doctoral programs in the "soft sciences" have a very difficult time finding suitable positions after graduation. In 1999 there were more than 140 universities offering a doctoral degree program in English. Only about a third of their graduates get tenure track jobs upon graduation. Others will struggle on holding part time teaching positions or temporary assignments. It is very obvious that a drastic cut in the production of Ph.D.s in English is in order, but it doesn't appear to be happening soon. Meanwhile American industry cannot fill the positions in the hard sciences and engineering created by the industrial growth. Some high-tech companies are offering a $10,000 bounty to their employees if they successfully help recruit a qualified acquaintance to join the firm. Native talent is in such a short supply that American companies are forced to resort to importing trained scientists from foreign lands.

Of the 6,369 Ph.D.s in engineering granted in 1996 fewer than 45 percent went to American citizens.[11] Today, significant percentage of professors of engineering, physics, chemistry and other hard sciences at American universities are foreign born. It is possible to find colleges of engineering in the U.S. where most, if not all, of the department chairmen are native Chinese.

11   *The Chronicle of Higher Education,* Aug. 27, 1999.

Without foreign scientists working in America's industrial research laboratories and universities, the economic miracle would soon evaporate. For instance, almost a third of Silicon Valley scientists are Asian born. In 1999 the quota to admit high-tech workers with three-year H-1B visas was set at 115,000. Industry clamored for many more. Indian or Chinese-born engineers created 27 percent of the over 4,000 high tech businesses founded in the years between 1991 and 1996. Industrial leaders as well as university presidents know this. They are keenly aware that the country desperately needs new talent to fill the voids. There are plenty of places in colleges and universities for freshmen who want to study strategically important subjects to help America became self sufficient in science and engineering.

It is a sobering thought that while professors of American universities won the lion's share of the Nobel Prizes in science in 1999 — four of the five winners in chemistry, economics, physics and medicine were professors or former professors of American institutions — *every one of them was born outside the United States.*

The rapidly growing need for engineers in America is exemplified by comparing two of the biggest engineering projects in the twentieth century. The building of the Hoover Dam, completed in 1936, required 5,213 full-time workers, with no more than a couple of hundred engineers among them. The completion of the Windows 2000 software program employs 5,345 full-timers, nearly half of them engineers.

Another difficulty endemic to universities is faculty inertia. No matter how brilliant an idea a college president or his advisors come up with, changing a college curriculum is fraught with difficulty. Following age-old rules of the academic world, faculty committees take hold of the matter and talk it to death. Hence, it is remarkable that graduate programs, for example in Library Science, have been transformed at many institutions into "Information Science," relying on computers and the Internet. This, of course, happened only after enrollments at Library Science programs had dropped precipitously over several years. It will be interesting to watch what will happen in the field of dentistry, for instance. Fluoridation of the drinking water from the 1960's helped raise a generation without cavities. Already some dental surgeons have encroached into the field of plastic surgery, doing face-lifts, much to the chagrin of medical doctors. Apparently, cutting back on an academic offering is rarely an option at our universities.

In the near future, the whole higher education system will experience a huge transformation. Its cause will be the Internet. Scholarly magazines are brimming with articles about its effect on teaching, the university structure, the whole system of credentialing. New academic programs are being devised to deliver academic "contents," even some new colleges have been created to utilize the digital format. Even major universities are testing the waters. The University of Maryland, for instance, offered degrees through the Internet for several years. Duke University has an excellent international business program for people with a minimum of ten years' experience. Columbia's graduate engineering programs offer degrees in six fields. Stanford, the University of Texas in Dallas, Northern Colorado, and the University of Phoenix are only a few of those schools that entered on-line teaching. However, it is not likely that "distance learning," as it is called, will truly make its impact soon. The problem is that today's technology is insufficient. One can not download, let alone participate interactively in, on-line academic work with modems currently in use. Newer technologies are a great deal faster, but only 3 percent of America's homes have cable modems, and only one percent was equipped with digital subscriber line (DSL) in the year 2000.

Scientists assure us that virtually free and practically infinite bandwidth telecommunications, petabytes of digital storage and scalable vector graphics, are near-term possibilities. What do they mean in plain English? That the contents of the entire Library of Congress plus the whole collection of the Smithsonian Institution in three-dimensional, animated pictures could soon be downloaded in a second into a digital storage device the size of a matchbox. This spells the death-knell of the present method of delivering knowledge. Gone will be the 50-minute lecture, fifteen classes a week mode of teaching. The whole system of higher education will change drastically. College life as we know it will come to an end, but humanity always adapted. These days we fight wars with laser-bombs, but mediaeval forts still stand, reminding us of wars past. Similarly, after a long while, the huge complexes of auditoriums, residence halls, libraries and administration buildings will remain, empty and forlorn, reminding us of the time when junior mandarins were trained in them for four years. "Imagine, four out of five of them didn't even take a single course in physics" people will say.

3. Our Leading Schools

The United States Department of Education recognizes over 3,800 institutions of higher education. The criteria for recognition include the requirement that an institution be accredited by an agency that is recognized by the government.

There are two levels of accrediting agencies: regional and professional. Regional agencies accredit the institution; professional accrediting agencies accredit each academic program. For instance, a university located in Pennsylvania, has to seek accreditation from the North Central Association of Colleges and Schools. Once such accreditation is requested, the agency inspects the institution from top to bottom, evaluating the academic programs, the library, all other facilities, faculty, administration, rules and regulations, the lot. Once a school gains its initial regional accreditation, it must be renewed periodically.

A new professional program has to operate for a period of time and should graduate its first group of students before it qualifies for its initial accreditation. Before the first visit by the accrediting agency, voluminous paperwork is generated to demonstrate every aspect of the academic program. Not only the required courses, but the day-by-day lecture outlines of each course, examples of graded homework, specimens of tests and final examinations classified under each grade given, are assembled to show the quality and quantity of the work by the students required to obtain a degree. Members of the visiting committee sent by the accrediting agency are senior professors at other, well established institutions, or representatives from the industry. They spend two to three days on site, carefully distributing and planning their work, studying the facilities, library holdings, classrooms and laboratories. They interview the members of the faculty, the administration and the students. Their report, completed after a few months, is sent to the accrediting agency and to the institution at the same time, asking for comments and corrections. When there are weaknesses in the program of the department, it may get only a short period to improve before it is revisited. Full accreditation, usually for six years, is a sign that all things are well. An academic program that is weak often receives a "show cause" why its accreditation should not be revoked. This is a most serious matter. A university can not expect to get many students if its programs are not regionally and professionally accredited.

Receiving full accreditation without any negative comments is not necessarily good for a department. If all is well, then the administration of the university will concentrate its resources on the weaker components of the institution. This is not to the advantage of other departments. So, to get something out of this arduous process, the head of the department and the dean of the college build a strong case to be used against the university administration to fix something that, in fact, is not broken. They ask for a once-in-a-lifetime windfall of resources, a big cut out of the general funds, under the threat that the department may lose its accreditation without the extra support. A few additional faculty members, a new laboratory, more space—whatever can be contrived under a given situation. Using the national, professional accrediting agency against one's own administration—and yet appearing to be a loyal member of the university—is a well honed (but sometimes dangerous) weapon in the hands of a department chairman. Members of the accrediting committee know this trick quite well. Usually they play their part in support of a department, giving little hints to the president and provost of the institution that not all is well.

Commonly it is the first degree, often the bachelor's degree, that is accredited in a professional field. Graduate, master's or doctoral degrees are usually not accredited by anyone. Interestingly, many liberal arts degrees are not accredited at all, although recently a group of some 15 universities joined forces to develop common standards.

One of the first thoughts of a parent about the prospects of a college-bound child is a nearby, small, reputable private college with cosy, homelike atmosphere offering a "good education." What one means by this is somewhat debatable, but will be somewhat clarified as more and more comparative information unfolds on these pages. There are several magazines, *U.S. News and World Report, Newsweek, Time* magazine's *The Princeton Review, Kiplinger's* and others that publish college rankings each year. They all use different criteria to rank universities, some of which are rather complex statistical works. These surveys have several faults. One, they select, for example, 100 of the best schools when there are over 3,600 two- and four-year colleges and universities that are fully accredited, fewer than three percent of the accredited colleges and universities. Overall there are some 6,000 institutions of higher education that accept students, and for many applicants any one of these could be quite appropriate. Of the 270 million citizens of the United States, about 1.61 million enter colleges as freshmen each year. There may be another million or so who consider college but—at least for the time being—decide against it. Publishing a list of the, say, 100 best (?) schools is not very helpful, except for the schools listed. However, it does sell magazines.

The relative ranking of various professional programs, on the other hand, is hard to find. Suppose one wants to study "plastics" after watching the 1960's hit movie, *The Graduate.* It isn't generally known that the top three schools in the field of polymer science in the United States are Case Western Reserve University, the University of Akron and the University of Massachusetts at Amherst. Who would guess, for instance, that Texas A&M, way out in cow country, has one of the three strongest academic programs in coastal engineering in the nation? Nobody imparts this type of information, although these are the really important things.

Obviously, when a good education is sought, the first question should be: "In what field?" A person who wants to be an accountant had better seek a school with a topnotch business college. There are fewer than 300 universities with an accredited College of Business Administration, although some 1,400 institutions offer bachelor's degrees in this field. Likewise, there are fewer than 400 universities with an accredited College of Engineering. The undecided student who has no clue what he or she would like to get a degree in four years later at the time of graduation, will have grievously limited choice of career if he or she starts out in a comfy small college.

Small colleges often offer degrees called pre-something. Let us take, for instance, an undergraduate pre-med degree. Ostensibly it includes a number of chemistry and biology courses required for admission at a medical school. Most medical students who flunk out of the program fail to pass courses in organic chemistry. The best training in this area is found in departments of chemistry and chemical engineering. As a matter of fact, chemical engineering graduates are usually sought-after applicants at medical schools. The question becomes, if the graduate with a pre-med background fails to gain admission to medical school, what is he or she prepared to do for a living?

A note of warning is due here. Some law school admission officers around the country apparently have no idea about the difference between a straight A background in basket-weaving and a B - in physics. As a result, America has a lot of lawyers with the undergraduate background of the former. But America has a lot of lawyers, period. This would be a tremendous competitive advantage on the international scene only if a country could sue itself to greatness.

One way to sort colleges and universities is by the size of the student body. Below is a table describing America's accredited institutions according to size of enrollment. It was composed from data collected by the U. S. Department of Education based on a survey made in the fall of 1996 of 3,278 accredited American higher educational institutions. The data excludes for-profit institutions, but includes 1,211 two-year colleges.

Reviewing the data one may note that the average university enrollment is between 1,000 and 2,500 for private, non-profit universities and between 2,500 and 5,000 for public institutions. There are more than 1,000 accredited private universities with enrollment smaller than one thousand, and about 550 public institutions smaller than 2,500. These are than the "small" schools. There are, obviously, lots to choose from if one insists on a small school with an ostensibly home-like atmosphere. Once one selects those which are not a whole continent away, a relatively short list can be made within one's home state.

Another way to sort schools is by the degrees offered and the number of faculty members in each discipline. This is

Enrollment	No. of Public Institutions	No. of Private Institutions
30,000 or more	26	2
20,000 - 29,999	89	5
10,000 - 19,999	235	37
5,000 - 9,999	368	87
2,500 - 4,999	381	168
1,000 - 2,499	381	470
500 - 999	115	315
200 - 499	55	257
200 or less	28	292

Size of Enrollment at American Colleges

an important determinant of quality. Some disciplines are so broad that several faculty members have to be available to cover the field adequately. Comparing schools on this basis is a very useful measure. Another aspect that needs to be looked at is the student/faculty ratio for the whole college. Elite colleges have seven or eight students for each faculty member. Others have twice as many students for each professor. The size of library, meaning the number of books held, is also a good comparative measure. In selecting a school, the cost of tuition should be the last consideration. Unlike Wal-Mart, college costs are generally as negotiable at the time of admission as prices at a garage sale. Although the cost of tuition is firmly stated, few students pay the full fare. They are offered scholarships by the school's financial office depending on a number of factors like parents' income, number of siblings, where the applicant comes from, his or her race and so on.

It is notable in the previous table that there are more than 100 big state universities that have in excess of 20,000 students; 115, to be precise. Only seven private universities are of comparable size. These are the big research universities where there is a full "menu" of every imaginable discipline available for the students. Truly, the basic idea of "university" embodies the notion of advancing knowledge and creativity along all fronts. The more the university takes part in scholarly pursuits and scientific research, the greater the depth and richness of the undergraduate experience. In its truest sense, the university integrates teaching and research, as well as public service, into one commodity: knowledge. The big schools are not, as small schools' admissions officers sometimes claim, big, impersonal diploma manufacturing plants where undergraduates are only numbers like prisoners in the Gulag. They are productive intellectual centers where the creative juices are flowing. In support of this notion, the table on the next page shows the 25 most productive universities and their incomes from royalties on patents generated by their faculty. Public institutions are shown in italics in the list. The data was compiled by the Association of University Technology Managers for fiscal year 1997. It includes the royalties received that year, the number of licenses generating these royalties, the number of patents issued, and the number of start-up companies formed.

There were more than 70 universities in America in 1997 that received over a half a million dollars in royalties in that year from patents generated by their faculty members, past and present. They are in the class of "research universities." These schools are the intellectual centers of the nation, where the inventions are created, and high technology

Research Universities	$ Royalties received	No. of Licenses generating royalties	Patents Issued in 1997	Start-up companies formed in 1997
U. of Calif. System	61,280,000	528	206	13
Columbia Univ.	46,105,192	201	43	4
Stanford Univ.	34,104,090	272	64	15
Florida State U.	29,901,112	11	10	1
M. I. T.	19,860,549	255	134	17
Mich. State U.	18,293,388	41	37	2
U. of Florida	18,156,198	255	47	0
U. Wisc. -Madison	17,172,808	41	69	2
Harvard Univ.	13,402,273	61	39	1
Carnegie Mellon U	13,381,000	133	4	3
Yale Univ.	13,054,287	232	24	1
U. of Washington	11,478,605	142	34	25
State U. New York	7,606,787	104	40	5
Iowa State Univ.	6,932,484	186	38	6
Tulane Univ.	6,640,800	18	6	0
Rutgers Univ.	6,489,874	191	25	7
Wash. Univ. MO	6,101,128	120	21	3
Baylor - Medicine	4,881,856	97	22	2
Johns Hopkins U.	4,686,519	103	37	3
Clemson Univ.	4,620,346	9	11	0
Univ. IL Urbana	4,091,329	122	20	n/a
Cal. Inst. of Tech.	4,056,829	45	40	9
Texas U. System	4,040,169	112	21	4
Cornell U. Res. Fd.	3,639,204	147	62	3

Income of Major Research Universities

start-up companies are formed. In the 24 universities shown in the table, over 126 companies were started using technologies covered by the patents assigned by their faculty inventors to the institutions. It obviously follows that these institutions had the resources and the infrastructure to develop these new technologies, with world-class laboratories, libraries, and computing facilities at hand, and, most of all, highly capable faculties and motivated, hard working, intelligent and capable students who worked with them. Often the inventors are students of the university rather than professors. The billionaire creators of Yahoo.com are just one example. Of the 24 universities listed, twelve are private institutions, and an equal number are state universities. This is a very interesting point: whether a school is public or private; quality apparently had nothing to do with such status.

The table on the previous page deserves a second look. The third column shows the number of patents that were licensed to corporations, and the the second column shows the income generated. The University of California system, including such notables as Berkeley and UCLA, had a total of 528 individual inventions by faculty members in the past. In the year of 1997 alone, 206 new inventions were patented. However, it is likely that they haven't yet produced any income. But, based on the reported 1997 inventions and those in the earlier years, 13 new companies were formed. These universities and other large universities like them are fueling the economic growth of the United States.

University research work often produces considerable income for the school and its faculty engaged in research. But few can be compared to the 1999 settlement in a lawsuit between the University of Minnesota and pharmaceutical giant Glaxco Wellcome. Professor Robert Vince's patent involving an anti-AIDS drug will bring in up to an estimated $ 300 million over ten years, representing ten percent of the U.S. sales of the drug.

The three top earners from licensed technology in 1998 were the University of California System with $ 73 million, Columbia University with $ 62 million, and Florida State University with $ 46.6 million. All but $ 1.6 million of the latter came from FSU's exclusive license to Bristol-Myers-Squibb to manufacture the popular cancer-fighting drug Taxol. In 1999 it was expected to bring in $ 60 million. In his 1993 book, *Earth in the Balance: Ecology and the Human Spirit,* Al Gore expressed his concern over the possibility that a California yew will be eliminated because it contained a cancer-fighting compound, taxol. Soon after that FSU professor Robert Holton synthesized Taxol, a triumph for modern chemistry. The yews are saved.

Science and technology research in universities sometimes causes unique situations. Yahoo founder Jerry Yang is a dropout from Stanford's Ph.D. program, where his former professors' average yearly salary is $ 95,000. Yang's net worth in 1999 was about $ 6 billion[1].

Research, meaning serious scientific research in the so called "hard" sciences, is the primary business of our best universities. The leading sponsor of this work is the Federal Government. Lots of money comes from industry, including foreign companies, but the major contributor is Uncle Sam. In 1997 the total U.S. spending on scientific research at 100 of the largest research universities of the country ex-

---

1   Much of this has evaporated in the subsequent demise of technology stocks.

ceeded $ 11.877 billion. That is eleven with nine zeros after it, a lot of dough. It included a wide range of scientific subjects, from cancer research to the effect of cattle-herds' flatulence on global warming. The ten busiest research universities, with their 1997 federal research grants, are:

- Johns Hopkins University - $ 724,526,000
- Stanford University - $ 332,272,000
- *Univ. of Washington -* $ 320,784,000
- MIT - $ 311,396,000
- *Univ. of Michigan -* $ 296,028,000
- *U.C. San Diego -* $ 274,860,000
- *U.C.L.A. -* $ 238,919,000
- *Univ. of Wisconsin, Madison -* $ 233,760,000
- *U. C. San Francisco -* $ 229,323,000
- Harvard University - $ 222,612,000

Even the lowest one on the list of 100 schools — according to the National Science Foundation — Dartmouth College, boasts a very respectable $ 43,145,000 a year. Hundreds of other university-based research facilities received federal funds. Does anyone wonder why research is the primary interest of our universities? Why professors' career interest is overwhelmingly research oriented? To quote bank robber Willie Sutton, "that is where the money is." An average full professor at Rockefeller University, a distinctly research-oriented institution, earned $ 125,400 in 1998-99. There were 19 institutions that year where the average salary of a full professor exceeded $ 100,000; they were all research universities. In contrast, three small liberal-arts colleges reported average full professor salaries under $30,000. The national average salary for assistant professors at research universities was $ 48,531 in that year, while colleges offering baccalaureate degrees paid only $ 38,599 at the same rank, according to a survey by the American Association of University Professors.

From the point of view of an applicant seeking a slot as a freshman at a big school, there are several positive and negative aspects. A positive one is that there is no limitation on the selection of a discipline. Everything is available. A negative aspect is that one is a tiny spot on a very large scene. Some students enjoy this, it gives them privacy. However, unless one wants to live like a hermit, living among a great variety of people is what life is about. The sooner a young person realizes this, the better.

Big universities offer such a great variety of courses that students can easily get distracted. It is a kid in the candy store situation. Focusing on one's educational goal is very important. It is really the job of the schools' academic advisors to keep their students on track, but sometimes they fail to do so.

Reading is the essence of higher education, rather than sitting through lectures, making notes, and taking examinations. The size of the library of an academic institution is one of the best measures of the quality of the educational experience of its students. The table across shows America's ten largest university libraries, the number of volumes they hold and the size of the library's yearly budget. The information is culled from the 1997-98 report of the Association of Research Libraries, published by *The Chronicle of Higher Education*.

Public institutions, as before, are shown in italics. Again, one may note that half of the top ten are public universities.

The size of a college library is less important in an urban setting, if there are other universities with sizeable libraries nearby. For instance, a small college in Washington D.C. may benefit from the many other institutions around it, in addition to the vast holdings of the Library of Congress which has almost 24 million books. In New York City, local universities' library holdings are augmented by the presence of the New York Public Library with almost 7.5 million books. The same is the case in Boston, where the public library contains 6.7 million books. But if one studies at a college that is way out in the sticks and the college library has fewer than perhaps 50 thousand volumes, it will be a disadvantage.

The Internet is rapidly changing all this. The February 12, 1999 issue of *The Chronicle of Higher Education* reported the results of a survey of history professors at 101 institu-

University Library	No. of Books Held	Yearly Library Budget, $
Harvard University	13,617,133	70,917,819
U. C. Los Angeles	7,010,234	37,007,887
Yale University	9,932,080	39,154,000
U. C. at Berkeley	8,628,028	33,933,812
U. Illinois, Urbana	9,024,298	25,314,119
Stanford University	6,865,158	42,954,263
U. of Michigan	6,973,162	34,273,593
Univ. of Texas	7,495,275	24,538,692
Columbia University	6,905,609	29,231,723
Cornell University	6,113,346	28,358,048
U. of Washington	5,715,202	27,030,473

The Largest University Libraries

tions. It stated that as many as 93 percent of the respondents used the Internet for scholastic research. Indeed, the number of full-size books available on the Internet is staggering. To the students this means that it is no longer a necessity to go off to a library, it is often easier to log onto the Web and run a search.

Another way of measuring the quality of universities is the number of doctorates granted in a given year. In 1997 the Survey of Earned Doctorates, published by *The Chronicle of Higher Education*, shows that the 20 largest universities producing doctors' degrees, with the number of degrees granted in the year, are:

- *University of Texas, Austin -* 787
- *University of Wisconsin, Madison -* 786
- *University of California, Berkeley -* 759
- *University of Illinois, Urbana - Champlain -* 736
- *Ohio State University -* 708
- *University of Minnesota, Twin Cities -* 708
- *University of California, Los Angeles -* 670
- *University of Michigan, Ann Arbor -* 642
- Harvard University - 593
- Stanford University - 591
- *Texas A&M University -* 544
- *Pennsylvania State University -* 542
- *University of Washington -* 526
- *Purdue University -* 509
- *University of Maryland, College Park -* 505
- Cornell University - 485
- Massachusetts Institute of Technology - 485
- Columbia University - 452
- *University of Arizona -* 445
- University of Pennsylvania - 441

As before, the schools in italics are the largest and best public institutions of the country measured by doctoral degree production in 1997, while six of the list are the country's best private schools.

Altogether there are 50 institutions in the nation that graduated 275 or more Ph.D.s in 1997. They are classed as the nation's "doctoral institutions." The remainder of the 3,800 universities grant two-year associate and bachelor's degrees, and in some cases, master's degrees. The faculty of this remaining class do little research, and probably not much publication. Whether they keep up with the growth of knowledge is often questionable. In the case of smaller schools, things get worse. Faculty members with fewer peers in their own specialty feel isolated and often deteriorate professionally when there is no one to match wits with about a common academic discipline.

The doctoral degree figures above lump together all fields, from arts and humanities to physical sciences. In 1997, for example, 42,705 doctorates were granted nationwide in the United States. The distribution of the fields was as follows:

- Arts and Humanities -   5,387
- Business and Management - 1,221
- Education -   6,497
- Engineering -   6,052
- Life Sciences -   8,213
- Physical Sciences -   6,574
- Social Sciences -   6,917
- Others incl. Professional fields - 1,844

The proportional distribution in 1997 between males and females receiving doctoral degrees ranged from 87 percent men versus 13 percent women in engineering to 36.4 percent men versus 63.6 percent women in education. As reported by *The Chronicle of Higher Education,* 58.5 percent of the total doctoral degree recipients were men.

In the foregoing, different measures were shown for evaluating and classifying universities. The first group shows the leading research universities. The second group lists the largest doctoral institutions. The schools mentioned here are only a sample from the top of their respective lists. These lists are to demonstrate the wide variety of colleges and universities where an undergraduate is likely to find the widest choice of academic disciplines. From this small survey the reader will get an impression how broad the opportunities are.

America's higher educational institutions are greatly respected throughout the world. Many students come from foreign lands. Foreign students studying in the United States bring a variety of important benefits to the nation. They spend a great deal of money here, on tuition, room and board, tourism and a variety of other ways. They learn English with an American accent, learn our way of life, establish lifelong friendships, and leave with an inclination to do business with contacts established in the United States. Other nations, France and Russia being leading examples, try to emulate this example and attempt to attract foreign students to their universities. As early as 1983, the Ministry of Education of Japan set up a plan to raise the number of foreign students in the country to 100,000 by the twenty-first century, in order to increase Japan's international influence. But America has an immeasurable lead; her competitors aren't doing all that well. Japan, for example, had only about 50,000 foreign students in 1998. In the 1997-98 school year, there were over 481,000 foreign students in America, spending an estimated $ 7.5 billion a year. In 1999, foreign students contributed $ 11 billion to the U. S. economy, about a tenth of the export revenues the tourist industry generated.[2] Britain is second with 200,000 foreign students, France is third with 130,000. Alas, the American advantage is decreasing. While in the past decade there was an 11 percent growth in the number of foreign students in the United States, the growth in Britain was 148 percent, in Australia 221 percent.[3]

Many foreign leaders are American educated. Japan's Empress Michiko, Pakistan's former Prime Minister Benazir Bhutto and French President Jacques Chirac are Harvard graduates. U.N. General Secretary Khofi Annan and former Israeli Prime Minister Benjamin Netanyahu are MIT graduates. Jordanian King Abdullah, the Sultan of Oman and Spanish Prince Felipe de Borbon all studied in the United States. As French Foreign Minister Hubert Vedrine put it: "Today, in all the world's governments you find people who were shaped by American universities. It is an instrument of power."

President Nixon's advisor Henry Kissinger's wizardry in foreign affairs was established while he was writing his doctoral dissertation in 1952 at Harvard. He was put in charge of a new program that was to provide him with an extraordinary network of contacts in capitals around the world. It was called the Harvard International Seminar. It brought together 35 bright and influential foreigners to spend the summer along the banks of the Charles River discussing politics, philosophy and history. For all concerned it was a memorable experience. After several summers, the

2   *Forbes*, July 24, 2000.

3   ibid.

program had brought Kissinger into personal contact with hundreds of up-and-coming foreign politicians, scholars and journalists, who would always be grateful to him for the stimulating July and August at Harvard. It is known today that the Harvard International Seminar was a CIA-supported ingredient of America's Cold War against Communism, a thought that makes neo-Bolshevik history professors at today's Harvard cringe.

According to a 1997 - 98 report made by the Institute of International Education, California had 65,292 foreign students[4] in its universities in the 1997-98 school year, New York State had 51,262, Texas 29,542, Massachusetts 27,121, Florida 21,096 and Illinois 20,703. Thirteen states had more than 10,000 each. Of these, 57.7 percent came from Asia, 14.9 percent came from Europe and 10.7 percent from Latin America. The rest came from the Middle East, Africa, and other places around the globe. Fifty-eight percent were men. About half of these students were undergraduates. In terms of their country of origin: Japan sent 47,073 students, China 46,958, Korea 42,890, India 33,818 and Taiwan 30,855. From Europe, Germany sent 9,309, Great Britain 7,534, Russia 6,424, France 5,992, Sweden 4,412 and Spain 4,371. Even ramshackle Bulgaria joined in with 2,265 students. If one considers that these students pay out-of-state tuition, about twice the regular cost — not

4   On America's colleges foreign students are
     referred to as "international students." As they
     do not come from the United Nations, this
     definition is silly educational jargon.

to mention overseas travel expenses — foreign students must value their American education.

These numbers are staggering. Assuming that an average university has, say, 5,000 students, then the state of California alone has enough foreign students to completely fill over 13 mid-size universities!

Surveys show that the primary academic interests of foreign students were business and engineering, 21 and 15 percent respectively. Others came to study mathematics and computer science (9 percent), physical and life sciences (8 percent) and social sciences (8 percent). They selected, of course, the best institutions: 41 percent studied at research universities, 14 percent at doctoral institutions and 19 percent at master's level institutions. Interestingly, 15 percent went to two-year colleges. Only five percent of the foreign students study at four-year bachelor's level colleges. One wonders why.

The concentration of foreign students at selected institutions is quite revealing: 18.8 percent of the student body at Harvard, 19.8 percent at Columbia, and 22.5 percent at the New School of Social Research (New York City) are foreigners. But even at the huge "Big Ten" schools of the Midwest a sizeable percentage of the students are from foreign lands:

- University of Michigan, Ann Arbor - 9.2 percent,
- Ohio State University, Columbus -   8.0
- Purdue University, West Lafayette - 9.1
- University of Illinois, Urbana -   8.6
- Michigan State University, Lansing - 6.6
- University of Wisconsin, Madison -   9.5

These foreign students make a significant impression on the culture of an institution. They provide a window to the world, a cosmopolitan atmosphere, a free learning experience to the American students, many of whom have not traveled much farther than the capitals of their respective states, or perhaps to Disney World in Orlando. In the new century when industry must think in global terms and the Internet's Worldwide Web offers infinite communication and global knowledge resources, international educational experiences are increasingly significant.

According to the Institute of International Education, about 9.3 percent of American college students study abroad for a semester or summer. Some 63.7 percent of them go to Europe, Britain, Spain, Italy and France being the most popular destinations. Universities sending the largest number of students to study abroad are Michigan State, Texas at Austin, University of Pennsylvania, Arizona, Wisconsin and Miami of Ohio — all sent over 1,000 students each in 1997-1998.[5]

Unfortunately the interest of Americans in foreign language studies and education in foreign lands declined after America won the Cold War. Fewer American faculty members apply for Fulbright scholarships that support education exchange programs, and federal support has been slashed by 20 percent recently.

A potential freshman applicant to the nation's colleges and universities should find the career choices of foreign stu-

---

5   *The Chronicle of Higher Education*, Dec. 10,
     1999.

dents quite interesting. They enter disciplines that are considered to be of value throughout the world. They study the stuff that made America great: business management, the "hard" sciences and engineering. They are the sons and daughters of the elites of other nations, what they want to take home is a piece of the American dream. Emulating them in their selection of schools and disciplines would seem to be a good idea.

4. College Output

In an ideal world a high-school graduate would be fully prepared to do college level work without remedial preparation in pre-college level mathematics, English, history, and physical and biological sciences. In fact, most of them aren't. Many students graduate from high schools without adequate reading comprehension or basic writing skills, let alone, for instance, a course in basic physics.

In an ideal world, students in universities would undertake studies that lead to careers needed by the nation, education, engineering, medicine, nursing and other health sciences, geology, chemistry, physics, accounting, law, journalism, drama, criminology, agriculture, biology, psychology and so on. Western cultural history, English and other fundamental courses should have been covered at the high school level. In an ideal world, these courses should not be a required part of the training of nurses, engineers, business management specialists and people in other fields that require rigorous state licensing to be admitted to practice. But in fact, these courses are required: Fully one-third of these programs consist of such "high-school remedial" courses.

In an ideal world, physicians, lawyers, dentists, pharmacists and other professionals could start their specialized education at the freshman level, rather than after they finish an unspecified undergraduate bachelor's level program, but they do not. Most professional disciplines wait four years, until their prospective students are weeded out by a selective process carried on by their undergraduate instructors in biology, mathematics, physics and chemistry. After all that pre-selection, few flunks out of medical school (if they do, most often organic chemistry causes it, a distinctly "under-graduate" course).

We do not live in an ideal world. After twelve years, high-schools do not prepare American youth for university level work. Essentially, after entering college students have to take about three semesters' worth of courses that have absolutely nothing with what they are to do in their future career. Although given many sly names — "general education requirements," "common core," etc.— they potentially serve only two purposes: either making up high school level courses or keeping some faculty groups fat and happy.

The General Education Requirement may typically include the following courses:

- English Composition: 2 courses, 7 credits minimum.
- Mathematics: 3 credits.
- Natural Science: 8 credits minimum, one of which to include a laboratory. [courses from the departments of Anthropology, Biology, Physics, Chemistry, Geology]
- Oral Communication (Public Speaking): 3 credits.
- Social Sciences: 6 credits. [courses from the departments of Economy, Government/Politics, Geography, Psychology and History]
- Humanities: 10 credits, 3 courses. [courses from the departments of Philosophy, Fine Arts, Classics and Literature]
- Area Studies/Cultural Diversity: 4 credits, 2 courses. [this used to be called Eastern Civilizations, or something to that effect, before it was dumbed down.]
- Physical Education/Wellness: 1 credit. [five week's instruction on how to play golf would satisfy this requirement.]

All this adds up to over 40 credits or about a third of the four-year academic program. How does the faculty come up with such a list? Through endless hours of meetings, in which representatives of every conceivable discipline insist that their own basic courses are by far the most important in a young person's general education. These courses generate a lot of credit hours for a department too. In essence, the whole thing means that three semesters of the four-year curriculum cover what used to be high school material some years ago. The result is that the really meaningful part of the undergraduate academic program is taught in two and a half years. The British practice of a strong high school followed by three-year degrees looks comparable when viewed from this point of view. The stated reason to require these fundamental courses is to assure that everybody with a diploma, in whatever field, has a smattering of fundamental knowledge, to make up for the sad state of America's high school education. Students, particularly those who didn't come to party but to get training for a career, do not appreciate the faculty's "concern" about their general education, but they have no input except the financial one. European universities have no such requirements. Their students, after they passed secondary school, enter with a basic education, which equals about three semesters' work in the United States.

At first glance the problem could be solved with relative ease: require college-bound high-school students to get better preparation in English, mathematics, history and science. To facilitate this, subsidize the training of capable high school teachers to teach the necessary courses and support high schools that enable their students to perform quality work.

Looking at the problem from the standpoint of the colleges, solving the problem gets trickier. Some faculty groups have

Academic Subject	% of Students Taken Courses
English Composition	68.9
Physical Education Activities	61.6
General Psychology	56.7
Literature and Letters	51.8
U.S. History/Civil War	40.3
Introduction to Sociology	39.2
General Biology	36.3
Philosophy and Religious Studies	33.7
Introduction to Economics	31.5
Business & Management	31.2
Intro. to Coll. Level Mathematics	30.9
U.S. Constitution, Government	29.0
General Chemistry	29.0
Western Civilization/ World History	24.6
Accounting	23.9
Music (not performing)	23.7
Calculus and Adv. Mathematics	21.0
Fine Arts	20.3
Anthropology/Archeology	19.5
Physics	18.0
Geology and Earth Science	17.3
Mathematical Statistics	13.7

Courses taken by undergraduates

a strangle-hold on their clientele. They insist on maintaining college-wide academic requirements that include their specialties. They consider themselves the ultimate repositories of essential knowledge. They hold the key to success — material as well as intellectual — of other people's live.

Freshmen enter college full of enthusiasm and anticipation, but scant knowledge of what they need or would like to study. Faculty members— *in loco parentis* —provide guidance. The outcome, courses taken and degrees obtained, depends as much on the will of the faculty as on the will of the students. So, what is the outcome of four years of study in an American college?

The National Longitudinal Study of the high school class of 1972, involving thousands of college students, have provides a glimpse of what courses college students are taking toward their degrees during their undergraduate years. The data showing the predominant courses appearing on students' transcripts is included in the table opposite.

This data reveals that America's college graduates in recent decades have been taking heavy doses of English writing and literature, psychology, sociology and even biology. But fewer than one in four took even a single a course in western civilization or world history, accounting, college level mathematics or statistics, or physics, not to mention more rigorous courses.

Let's now take a look at the bachelor's degrees produced by the nation's colleges and universities recently. The table on the following page shows the number of bachelor's degrees awarded in the 1995-96 academic year at American colleges and universities in major fields of study. Fields in which fewer than 10,000 bachelor's degrees were awarded, about 15 percent of the total, are excluded.

Group	Academic Field	BS/BA Degrees	%
A	Agriculture and Natural Resources	21,431	1.8
A	Biological and Life Sciences	60,994	0.5
B	Business and Marketing	227,102	19.
B	Communications	47,320	4.0
A	Computer and Information Sciences	24,098	2.0
B	Education	105,509	9.0
A	Engineering	62,114	5.3
C	English Language and Literature	50,698	4.3
A	Health Professions	84,036	7.2
C	Liberal/General Studies	33,997	2.9
A	Mathematics	13,143	1.1
n.a.	Multidisciplinary/Interdisciplinary Studies	26,515	2.2
A	Physical Sciences	19,647	1.7
B	Protective Services	24,818	2.1
C	Psychology	73,291	6.3
B	Public Administration and Services	19,849	1.7
C	Social Sciences and History	126,479	10.8
C	Visual and Performing Art	49,296	4.2
	All Academic Fields	1,164,792	100

Bachelor's Degrees granted in the United States in 1995 -1996

Admittedly it is somewhat arbitrary, but one may sort these fields into three broad groups. In Group A are academic fields that lead to careers involving "value added" productive work in science, research, technology, and agriculture, including the disciplines that lead to state licensure and recognized professional status.

Group B comprises supporting fields that are required to maintain the productive life of the nation, including education, protective services, administration, business management and communication. Most of the holders of these degrees end up with some type of certificate issued by a state. Group B fields do not necessarily generate wealth, but enable Group A fields to thrive.

Group C includes liberal arts, social sciences, history, political science, English, arts and psychology. They are nice things to study but in contrast to the other groups, they do not add materially to the well being of the nation. Possessing a B.A. degree in history implies high learning but qualifies a person for little more than an associate (clerk, in other stores) position at Wal-Mart.

Psychology is a case in point. Only a doctorate and some years of supervised experience qualify a person for a psychologist's license in most states. In the 1995-96 academic year, the same period when the bachelor's degrees shown above were granted, 13,792 master's degrees, and only 3,711 doctorates were granted in psychology. Does America really need 73,291 bachelor level "psychologists" every single year, so that five percent of them can be trained to be licenced Ph.D. psychologists? Barring a spectacular increase in graduate enrollment in the field, one can assume that the great majority of the psychology graduates remained at that academic level, or transferred to other academic disciplines for graduate work, (law school, for instance.) Holders of a bachelor's degree in psychology spend four or more years in college and make a hefty financial contribution toward the well-being of psychology departments at our nation's colleges, with not much to show for it.

Summing up the percentages for the various groups in the table one finds an interesting result: The percentages of the three groups almost perfectly match! Group A adds up to 28.8, Group B to 27.4, and Group C to 28.7. The three groups together amount to about 85 percent of the total number of bachelor degrees in 1995-96. The remaining 15 percent includes poorly defined interdisciplinary and minor fields of study.

Without any further splitting of disciplinary hairs, one may conclude that about one third of education in our nation's colleges and universities leads to degrees that are absolutely essential for the nation's well being and another third is definitely necessary for the maintenance of the country. The last third, hundreds of thousands of misguided American college students in every academic year, are taking courses in subjects that — albeit interesting, stimulating, educational, civilizing, sophisticating, cultivating and enriching — do not contribute to the daily survival of either the person or the nation.

From the point of view of an outside observer, colleges that churn out degrees in academic fields that have no apparent value on the marketplace are not as much involved in education as they are in running a racket. Harsh words. They contradict the common concept in the minds of parents: Ivy -covered faux-mediaeval halls filled with benevolent father-figures (or mother-images) laden with doctoral degrees and profound wisdom, taking over nurturing parental duties — albeit for a hefty compensation.

The problem for America arising from the misdirected emphasis in the undergraduate degree output of our colleges and universities was best described by syndicated columnist Charley Reese in a recent article:

"In the long run, I do not think that a nation of lawyers, stock salesmen, bankers, discount merchants, accountants and entertainers can stand against nations of engineers, industrialists and inventors. Substance beats fluff every time."

5. Administration

America's academia includes public and private schools to handle the 15.1 million undergraduate and graduate students. Aside from the federal service academies, public schools are state "assisted." The definition is important. In Europe most state universities are financed by the state, lock, stock and barrel. America's state colleges receive perhaps a third of their financial support from the state budget; the rest must be scraped together from tuition and fees paid by the students, donations from former graduates, the 'alumni', overhead on research contracts, royalty payments on licensed patents, federal grants of various kinds, donations from foundations, gifts, endowments, income on public service activities, sales of books and supplies, and a multitude of other sources. The state legislature pays a certain yearly operational support based on the number of undergraduate and graduate full-time students, calculated on the credit hours generated. This state subsidy supports students who are residents of the state. Out-of-state students pay the full fare. In addition to this, the legislature includes lump sum amounts for new buildings into the state's construction budget. Altogether, it is a huge amount: In the 1999 - 2000 state budgets, the total appropriation to finance United States universities was $ 56,683,511,000.

Non-profit private universities, much fewer in number, do not generally receive any state support. This is why private colleges are considerably more expensive than state "assisted" institutions. When considering college, one should keep in mind that state property and income taxes have already been sent to the state's colleges and universities. A student in a state university is getting some of his, or his parents' money back by utilizing the relatively cheap services provided.

Getting the money together to operate a college or university, whether a state institution or a private, non- profit one, is of crucial importance. This is the job of the members of the Board of Trustees. Hence the ultimate power at an American university rests with the Board of Trustees (alternatively called Directors, Visitors, etc.), an outside body appointed by the Governor in the case of state universities. The number of board members can be as few as ten or fewer to over 50. Harvard and many state institutions get along with few. Financially struggling small, private colleges need many board members. They are the moneybags. Recently, for example, Florida's small Eckerd College lost much if its endowment money through foolish investments. Its 54 wealthy board members soon raised over 16 million to make up the shortfall. Board members may be leading citizens, company presidents and other notables at best, or political cronies at worst. They serve a lengthy term, as much as eight years at some places. They receive little in return for their work, aside from the glory that shines on them from leading a lofty institution where they might not have been accepted as freshmen at the onset of their careers.

In America, Boards of Trustees operate just as boards do in industry. They are ultimately in charge of the running of the school, and running a college or university ultimately boils down to marshaling and allocating resources. A school's resources include manpower, space, time, books, equipment, repute and money. To run a university is much more than providing faculty and students with classrooms, equipment and books. Courses are to be scheduled, hallways cleared, catalogs printed, students admitted and registered, life and medical insurance and pensions managed, grass cut, snow removed, salaries paid, transcripts kept, parking supervised, offices assigned, rooms heated, purchases made, bills paid, and so on. Offhand, the performance and management of these important tasks is never quite appreciated by members of the faculty, who assume that chalk will appear on the blackboard by magic, but the numbers speak clearly: supporting the 550,000 full-time faculty members in the nation's colleges and universities there are more than 1.25 million administrators, clerical staff and maintenance people to keep the schools running, this is counting full-time personnel only.

For the day to day operation of the university, the governing board appoints the president. The board selects the president from a slate presented by a search committee composed of faculty, administrators and a couple of token students. The board also ultimately approves the budget, academic and personnel proposals and other sundry matters put to them from the Faculty Senate and other underlings.

The president of a college or university is its main booster, public representative, fund-raiser, administrative head and chief surrogate. He is Mr. University. He orchestrates the mission statements, conjures up the collective vision, and pushes the town-and-gown camaraderie, but basically his primary job is to keep the money flowing to the various operations of the university.

To be a president at an American university one does not have to be a scholar, but a very astute politician. Strength of intellect, scholarship and backbone are not sought after by presidential search committees. What counts is political skill in simultaneously catering to all campus constituencies, ranging from self-important, conceited tenured faculty to arrogant minority groups demanding their "rights." Academic qualifications of sitting presidents range widely. A few have a very solid academic background with significant research accomplishments, well regarded scientific publications, and many years of teaching. Others, the great majority, have flimsy backgrounds where scholarship is concerned, rather, their resumes are full of short, progressive positions in administration.This is fine, as long as they recognize this fact. There are a few presidents who do not. From this stems a great deal of the frequent acrimony between the faculty and the administration.

According to a recent survey, the typical[1] American university president is a white male in his fifties with a doctorate in education, or perhaps in the humanities, who was in a high administrative position elsewhere before he took the presidency. Alas, he has less than six years of experience as a full-time faculty member, indicating that early in his career he already had a driving ambition to get away from the classroom, even if it meant to work in some lowly paper-pushing position as assistant to a dean or something like that. The ideal, according to the much respected writer and academician, Jacques Barzun:

"It is the presence of golden aims – education itself and the ideal of public service — that makes it necessary for the administrator of higher rank to be a university man. He must, in fact, come "out of the classroom," and it is an advantage to him if he is also a respected scholar. The first requirement has a reason behind it: the emotions and standards of academic life still differ enough from those of business and the other professions to call for the ability to read the academic mind. Able executives from business or government find it hard to make out what will be congenial or tolerable or insulting to 'the professors'."[2]

1   *The Chronicle of Higher Education*, Aug. 27, 1999.

This presidency business is unique to America. In European countries, where state universities are not assisted but fully supported financially, the leadership is firmly in the hand of the senior faculty. They elect from among themselves and for a short period of time like four years, the *rector,* who is the leader of the university. He presides over a thin and generally powerless bureaucracy that handles the necessary paperwork but is fundamentally subservient to the faculty. They go back to their research and teaching after such service, happy to be rid of it. There is not much worry about finances; the money is sent down from the government's ministry of education or culture.

The presidential paycheck, in 1999, ranged from an average of $ 215,000 at a doctoral level institution to a bit over $100,000 at a two-year college. It is not a lot of money if one considers the amount of frustration and the degree of constant exposure that go with the job. Dealing with the prima donna faculty members inside and the gigantic egos of politicians and benefactors outside is a tough job. A wise old president remarked once that it is easier to move a cemetery than change a college curriculum. Thomas Sowell, writer and senior fellow at the Hoover Institution once wrote in an article entitled *Titanic Problems in Academia:*

"most of the big decisions are either made by the faculty or cannot be made over the opposition of the faculty. Moreover, the faculty knows that presidents come and go, while a full professor goes on like Old Man River." [3]

2   Jacques Barzun: *The American University,* New
     York: Harper & Row, 1968.

3   *Forbes,* Nov. 30, 1998

Universities up to the 1960s were quite different from today. The administration, in concert with the faculty, was in full control in the past. The academic quality of programs was significantly higher than today. Even though a purely liberal arts education often did not have a great deal of economic value, its academic content was assuredly firm. Today, in contrast, one can obtain a B.A. degree in English from a "high quality" college without ever taking a course on Shakespeare.

The pivotal turning point, when administrative — and academic — control of America's universities was lost can be traced to a cataclysmic series of events at Cornell University, according to professor Walter Berns. The assault on the universities by the Left began with violent student revolts in the 1960s. Berns explains:

"Shortly after he was installed as Cornell's president in 1963, James A. Perkins formed a Committee on Special Educational Projects charged with recruiting black students whose SAT scores were substantially below (as it turned out, 175 points below) the average of Cornell's entering class. Subsequently it was revealed that many of these students were to be recruited from the slums of the central cities, and perhaps not surprisingly, they proved incapable of being, or were unwilling to be, integrated into or assimilated by the Cornell student body; assimilation, they said, threatened their identity and needs as blacks.

"In 1966 they formed an Afro-American Society, which in short order demanded separate living quarters, an Afro-American studies program and seized a university building to house it and ultimately an autonomous degree-granting college. To justify it, they issued a statement saying that "whites can make no contribution to Black Studies except in an advisory, non-decision making or financial capacity" and therefore that the program must be developed and taught by blacks and, as it turned out, only to black students.

"This demand for an autonomous, degree-granting college took the form of an ultimatum, to which President Perkins responded by saying that he was "extremely reluctant to accept this idea of a college exclusive to one race, but [that he was] not finally opposed to it; it would involve a lot of rearranging of [his] personality." To head this college, or as it came to be known, this Center for Afro-American Studies, the university, without the consent of the faculty, hired a twenty-eight-year-old graduate student in sociology at Northwestern University who, despite repeated requests, failed to submit a statement explaining the center's purpose and operation. (The closest thing to a statement of purpose came from the Afro-American Society, which said that the aim of the center "would be to create the tools necessary for the formation of a black nation.") To teach the first course of the program (on "black ideology"), the university, over the objection of two (and only two) faculty members of the appropriate committee, hired a twenty-four-year-old SNCC (Student Nonviolent Coordinating Committee) organizer who had completed a mere two years of college.

"This jettisoning of academic standards, respecting the courses to be taught and the faculty to teach them, was largely the work of various members of the administration, only one of whom (the vice provost) was honest enough to admit that it was being done under pressure from the Afro-American Society but, he assured the few dissenting members of the faculty, "it would never be done again." To refuse to accommodate the black "moderates," he said, would only strengthen the hands of the 'militants'.

"Within a few months these 'moderates' were burning buildings; joining with the SDS (Students for a Democratic Society) to barricade Chase Manhattan bank recruiters; removing furniture from a women's dorm and placing it in a building taken over by the Afro-American Society; disrupting traffic; overturning vending machines; trashing the library; grabbing President Perkins and pulling him from a podium (and, when the head of the campus police rushed to Perkins's aid, driving him off with a two-by-four); harassing campus visitors with toy guns; and, at five or six o clock of a cold morning, seizing the student union building, driving visiting (and shivering) parents from their bed-rooms – it was Parents Weekend – out into the street. Justification for this seizure was said to be the burning of a cross on the lawn of a black women's dorm, which, the university now implicitly admits, was done by the "moderate" blacks themselves. They then brought guns – real, not toy, – guns into the student union and, two days later, at gunpoint, forced the university to rescind the mild (very mild) punishment imposed on the blacks found guilty of these various offenses by the student-faculty Committee on Student Affairs; in effect, they took control of the university. Photographs of the arms-bearing blacks, led by Thomas W. Jones, and of Vice President Steven Muller signing the surrender document appeared on the covers of the leading national news magazines." [4]

In Jeremy Rabkin's words:

"The most striking thing about the sixties, was that so much defiance and rebellion could emerge amid so much prosperity and security. The sixties were above all a revolt of the privileged and the overprivileged. That is why it was so much a matter of fantasy and escapism – of dressing up. Adolescents rebelled against their parents by refusing to cut their hair. Student radicals directed most of their rebellious animus against university administrators – for the most part mere bureaucrats with archaic titles ("provost," "dean") who turned out to be the most spineless "authority" figures in the whole country. A few steadfast administrators, like President Edward Levi at the University of Chicago, actually called in municipal police against students who were occupying and 'trashing' administration buildings." [5]

4   Walter Berns: The Assault on the Universities:
Then and Now, in *Reassessing the Sixties*
(Stephen Macedo, editor) New York: W.W.
Norton, 1997.

Soon after these events, academic and administrative controls were collapsing at other universities. Following the example of arrogant black militants, other "oppressed minorities," feminists, homosexuals, Hispanics, and Native Americans, demanded their share of the academic pie. Thirty years after, we have a plethora of courses stroking the tender ego of groups of self-proclaimed victims with no academic content whatsoever. As a logical consequence, it would not be surprising if additional "oppressed minorities" soon demand recognition, universal approbation, even celebration: necrophiliacs, pedophiliacs and the pederasts of NAMBLA, a group that "celebrates the joys of men and boys in love."

Navigating though these academic shoals is a perilous endeavor. As a safety feature, whenever a college administrator of whatever rank is appointed, he also receives a professorial position—on a tenure track or with tenure in some cases—in the department closest to his or her academic background. This is sort of an escape hatch, or a parachute. If the person doesn't work out in the administrative position he or she will "decide to return to teaching."

As an irritated president once remarked, the faculty, grouped into their academic departments are "a bunch of independent little fiefdoms." For professors, self-governance, independence and academic freedom are highly worshiped concepts, not to by trifled with by administrative or legislative types. Administratively, the traditional arrangement

5   Jeremy Rabkin: Feminism: Where the Spirit of
     the Sixties Lives On; in: *Reassessing the Sixties,*
     op. cit.

starts with the College of Arts and Sciences. It houses a disparate group of mathematicians, physicists, geologists, linguists, historians, and English departments — it is a microcosm in itself. Others are the Colleges of Business, Engineering, Nursing, Fine Arts and so on, each headed by a dean. The deans, who are under the leadership of the Provost, fight each other for sharing resources that are always short, and jointly fight the administration.

Deans are usually former department heads either in the same university or from elsewhere. They all have very respectable academic accomplishments, doctorates in their fields, published research results, textbooks, monographs and years of teaching experience. All are waiting for retirement or an occasional vice presidential appointment elsewhere. They lord it over a group of departments within their respective fields, each headed by a chairman or department head. The distinction is important: chairmen (chairpersons or chairs!) are elected by their faculty for a certain number of years. Department heads are appointed and "serve at the pleasure of the president." Big difference. A chairman is always mindful to have the voting faculty behind him; his peers could vote him out next year. The department head needs only the support of his academic superiors, the dean, the provost and the president. Of course, good politics require that he keep the support of his faculty colleagues. As in today's world, every academician is a specialist in his or her narrow topic, individual interests are widely divergent. Vicious office politics is always just under the surface.

With the constant growth of knowledge, the idea is that a department, as a producer of knowledge, has certain obligations to the profession. In historian Jacques Barzun's words:

"A department feels an obligation to cover the entire field as before; hence it must hire more persons, each doing less. Not all can be on tenure, so visiting professors become a regular element in the staff. Failing visitors, adjuncts can be borrowed for one course from a neighboring institution, at least for a year or two. Keeping the department up to full strength is therefore a never-ending task. Add the need to replace those who resign or retire, who die or who go on leave, and the *business* of a department, as distinguished from its profession, becomes as anguishing as playing the stock market. The business is at the same time much more expensive than before, owing the necessary trips, calls, letters, and meetings. For "the department" is no longer the chairman alone but a democratic machine embracing a search committee for beating the bushes and an executive committee for ratifying their choices." [6]

Life in academia is highly politicized. Under the polished veneer, there is constant, acrimonious, competitive infighting. Departments campaign for enlarging their academic turf, getting a larger share of the resources, more faculty, more space, more equipment, more graduate assistants, more of everything.To paraphrase Russia's Catherine the Great: a department is like a pumpkin, if it stops growing, it rots, so the departments argue about the establishment of new courses and additional areas of academic sub-fields that needed to be staffed by additional faculty qualified to teach the subject. The new areas of academic interest are supposedly to bring in additional students and resources: laboratory equipment, additional space, new research. And since the size of the financial pie is rather limited, the growth of each department comes out of the collective hide of another departments. Students of a politically powerful

6   Op. cit.

department end up with better laboratories, more qualified teachers, ultimately a better education.

After serving at the institution for a certain number of years — e.g. four or five — a faculty member either is given a terminal year of employment or is granted tenure. A tenured professor is assured a teaching position until retirement, unless he is convicted of some high crime or misdemeanor. Just by doing a miserable job at teaching, or not cracking a professional journal for decades, or not even thinking of looking for a research contract and rarely coming to the office does not fully qualify for dismissal. Such behavior patterns have to be painstakingly documented over a period of time before there are enough well-documented facts to get rid of a tenured professor. It is often better to wait until his retirement, while keeping his yearly raise as low as possible. (He or she may say that with the salary as low as it is, retirement is not an option.) America's colleges are more full of deadwood than her federal forests.

Tenure is the curse of American higher education. Originally it was invented to protect faculty members from the vagaries of politics, inside or outside of the university. It was an assurance of intellectual freedom. Today it generally protects the incompetent. There is a slow movement in American academia to introduce periodic reexaminations of tenured faculty. There are some universities, particularly at medical schools, where an alternative is offered to tenure track positions: three-year renewable contracts at higher salaries, for instance. But in general, no self-respecting professor would accept a position without the assurance that at a certain time in his future a tenured contract will be forthcoming.

To protect tenure and other faculty rights and perquisites, the faculty at some universities join unions. Usually the establishment of a union starts from some serious alleged grievance committed by the administration against the faculty. After a great deal of campus-wide acrimony a vote is held on the matter. Conservative departments, usually the colleges of business, engineering, nursing and others that offer economically valuable diplomas, tend to vote against the union. Others like sociology, education, fine arts, and political science, whose practitioners have few marketable skills outside of the university, are often for it. Once it is decided (not too often) that a union is to be set up, there is a rush from the outside. Usually the national organizations like the AFT, NEA, American Association of University Professors (AAUP) or, for instance, the Teamsters Union, rushes in to get a foothold. If in the final vote the faculty is unionized, the right to tenure is cast in stone, so is the assured yearly raise. Faculty members are not compensated anymore according to their performance. The union sets yearly raises based on rank and years of service. The institution's drive for academic excellence plunges. The administration, now including deans and department heads, is locked in an adversary relationship against the faculty union, as their interests diverge starkly. And in case of a strike, the president may find his house blockaded by burly truck drivers with an attitude. At the time of application, a prospective student is well advised to ask about whether the faculty is unionized. If so, keep away.

After the administration and the faculty, the third estate in the university triangle are the students. In mediaeval times they joined forces and hired their professors. Today, in America, they are the consumers of the $ 200 billion business of higher education. Gone are the days when they occupied the president's office at some of the Ivy League institutions of the country like Brown and Cornell, or wrecked the whole downtown, as at Kent, Ohio, demanding that the U.S. get out of Cambodia, or wherever. Now, within the university organization, students, as individuals, are rather powerless.

A unique aspect of financing a university in America is college sports. University administrators are keenly aware of the public relations value of intercollegiate athletics. How ingrained athletic competition is in the American psyche is demonstrated by the universal classification of the best universities of the land by their football league: Ivy League, Big Ten and so on. In Europe not even the news of a mud-wrestling championship among the College of Cardinals would be more inconceivable than a soccer match between the Sorbonne and Oxford. In America a game between the Buckeyes and Boilermakers is serious news. Regardless of how artificial the whole thing is, team sports are heavy stuff. They build college spirit, raise the number of applications, bring back alumni with their checkbook, and convince taxpayers – 80 percent of whom hold no college degrees – that financing the university is a wise investment. The State of Indiana, for instance, built a four-lane expressway in West Lafayette to connect Purdue University's football stadium with the nearby interstate highway. It makes the fans move faster during Homecoming Week festivities. Nothing is too expensive for Hoosiers when it comes to their beloved universities. In some states like Texas, Florida and others, college sports is almost synonymous with religion. In fact, the sight of kneeling football players praying to God for victory before a game is not uncommon.

Athletics are big business for colleges, the media and players. Universities with big athletics programs spend huge amounts of money to maintain them. Michigan State University, for example, recently built a $ 6.5 million 31,000 square-foot academic center for its athletes. Equipped with 62 computer workstations, a 210-seat auditorium and numerous meeting rooms, it is staffed with tutors virtually around the clock. Trying to keep players academically qualified and on track for graduation is the central purpose.

Big money is involved. For example, 85 percent of the budget of NCAA basketball is bankrolled from its eight-year, $1.7 billion television contract with CBS that expires in 2002. Another example, the "Final Four" college basketball games each year bring about $ 25 million income to the town hosting them.

For the players, college is the hope of entry to professional sports with its astronomic salaries and chance at lucrative advertising contracts with sneaker manufacturers. For the players working on their degrees and being on the team at the same time is very hard. Maintaining their eligibility is particularly difficult for those students who entered with already marginal qualifications. Athletes' academic performance and graduation rates worry administrators. Of the basketball recruits at the University of Connecticut, only 29 percent graduated between between 1994 and 1997. At Ohio State, another basketball powerhouse, only 31 percent of the players graduated, none of them was African-American. In all college competitive sports the national graduating rate of players is 41 percent. The chance to make it into professional sports isn't that great either. For most Division I basketball players, the chance to get to the NBA is less than one-half of one percent. Very few of the college athletes ever graduate with degrees in professional fields. But what intercollegiate sports has to do to with a college's educational function is questionable. The schools wring out millions of dollars of entertainment value from their athletes each year. Enthused alumni and state legislatures (often full of alumni lawyers) loosen the purse-strings for their *alma mater.* Brimming with college spirit, students go on a rampage, burning cars and breaking shop-windows when their school's team loses – as happened at Michigan State after losing the 1999 semi-final basketball tournament game. What does all this have to do with getting an education and earning a degree? Absolutely nothing.

6. The Professorate

In a modern university, according to author Charles Sykes:

"the various disciplines can be thought of as academic villages, complete with elders, wise men, and elaborate rituals of initiation and ostracism. They communicate through journals, conferences, books, papers monographs, as well as through peer review committees, professional organizations, and formal reviews of grant applications. Although they have no formal hierarchy, they control the informal hierarchy of status, reputation and prestige." [1]

Universities may have boards and presidents, provosts and deans, the academic control is firmly in the hands of the faculty. The administration is largely impotent. The true centers of power and authority are focused not in the administrative hierarchies but in the disciplines themselves. The primary concern and interest of faculty members is their connections to their peers at other institutions, rather than to their fellow professors at sister departments of their own institution. In their passion to protect faculty rights and academic freedom, there is little consideration of the rights of students, who are often victimized by the faculty.

Students view their professors as fountains of knowledge, people who dedicated their life to doling out arcane scholarship to all comers. After all, they went through graduate school, did some advanced research into their specialized

1   Charles J. Sykes: *ProfScam: Professors and the Demise of Higher Education*, Washington, D.C.: Regnery Gateway, 1988.

fields, wrote doctoral dissertations and passed complex examinations in order to have the "union card," the Ph.D., allowing them to enter the revered field of teaching. Now, one would think, they must be happy as larks that they found the Holy Grail, and at last their chance to teach. Wrong.

The Ph. D. stands for *doctor of philosophy,* the ancient terminology of mediaeval European institutions for the highest order of diploma that could be obtained. It was supposed to mean that its holder had all the knowledge humanly possible in his subject matter. The literary meaning of *philosophy* is defined as the "the critical study of the basic principles and concepts of a particular branch of science." The archaic meaning of *doctor* is a "man of great learning." We are caught up in a vast inflation of titles in America. A dentist is now called "doctor" and "deans" are dime a dozen at universities, in mediaeval times, only one went with each cathedral. One may get an eerie feeling that the classical concept is slowly debased as hundreds of universities grind on with their graduate programs offering an ever-widening array of doctoral programs.

There is a decisive difference between undergraduate learning and graduate school. Undergraduates are taught, particularly in the sciences, to learn the "truth," as it is written down in the textbook. It is dogmatic learning, particularly in the professional fields. Such training, at least at the undergraduate level, focuses on performing certain routine activities correctly — according to a widely accepted, prescribed rule, or legally set code in some cases — no alternatives are to be considered. Liberal arts students aren't exposed much to this type of teaching. They are given a much greater latitude for independent thinking. This is one of the strengths of liberal arts programs.

Graduate programs in the professional fields turn this approach around. Students are re-trained to question the dogmas. But the effects of the undergraduate approach lingers. Dogmatic learning is particularly acute in American universities. Once a visiting professor from London's Imperial College giving a seminar at Midwestern university started by admonishing his graduate student listeners that he expected vigorous arguments from them in case they did not agree with him. He explained that his students in Britain would tell him "what you say, professor, is nonsense" if they thought so. The seminar went on nicely, without any comments from the audience. If the professor wanted his listeners to *think* about what he lectured on, he did not succeed. Heavens! Who would ever question his wisdom?

At the graduate level, particularly in the doctorate program, the emphasis is on the "proof." The truth, the dogma, learned in the undergraduate program, is now questioned. It is taken apart, examined, and accepted only as long as it stands up to more fundamental scientific principles. The doctoral candidate has to go through this wrenching reevaluation of everything previously learned.

As people get older, they became ever more set in their ways. While in their twenties, graduate students accept these changes and adopt the inquisitive mentality necessary for original research. Most older people, those entering graduate school in their thirties and later, do not adapt well to these changes. They may get their degrees, but their mentality often remains set in the ways learned a decade or so before. While age-related discrimination is against the laws of the United States, academic hiring committees are aware of the fact that a younger candidate is often better, so they find some other attribute, a few courses that the younger applicant has taken in some field that is "desperately needed for the curriculum of the department," for instance. This swings the vote in the right direction. If there is a will, there is a way, a legal one.

Studying for a doctoral degree is all about research. A typical graduate program involves a collection of courses selected in such a manner that they provide the foundation for one's research topic, and its related major and minor academic fields. Traditionally, there is a major field and one or two minors. For instance, if one is majoring in astrophysics, mathematics and astronomy are logical minor fields. Generally, there can be no such thing as a minor unrelated to the research topic.

In the past, there was a requirement that the candidate pass qualifying examinations in two foreign languages. Not one, two. Knowing Americans' aversion to foreign languages, this was a rather silly rule. Still, the language of science before World War I was German and the language of diplomats was French, so it all made some sense at one time. But such knowledge was most often skin-deep. This writer recalls a story of a friend, a doctoral candidate in economics at a huge Midwestern school in the late 50's, who spoke several languages fluently. When he visited the professors of German and French to discuss his language requirements, he spoke to them in colloquial German and French. He found that neither of them spoke their respective languages. Yet they were the ones who passed judgment on all doctoral students' language knowledge.

As time passed, the language requirement was changed at some schools to accept a computer language in place of one foreign language. In retrospect, it was a rather dumb idea. Learning computer programming languages like BASIC or FORTRAN was a great deal less work than learning a real language. Most computer applications today are so user-friendly that there is no use whatsoever for computer programming as long as it is not someone's tool to make a living. With the increasingly global involvement in most walks of professional life, requiring just one language, but insisting on really mastering it, would be a useful doctoral requirement. But it is tough to demand something from the degree candidates that virtually none of the professors themselves is capable of doing. Hence the language requirement is fading. Most of our better universities claim today that their faculty is composed of 95 % or more Ph.D.s. If the traditional foreign language requirement were just halfway enforced, we would have far fewer Ph. D.s running around.

The doctoral research, at least in traditional theory, should advance the cutting edge of science. The recipient of the doctorate — again, at least according to the tradition — should know the most in the whole world about the tiny portion of his or her field discussed in the dissertation. As it used to be said in jest: "To know more and more about less and less, until one knows absolutely everything about nothing." But to give research and doctoral level institutions their due, doctoral graduates are probably exceptionally well trained in their scientific disciplines. But can they teach it?

In the preparation of a young Ph. D., not a single required course has anything to do with teaching. The candidate for a degree gets his teaching experience by teaching a few undergraduate courses in his field, assuming he is hired as a teaching assistant. Those who went through their graduate program as research assistants don't even have this minuscule teaching experience.

A newly-minted Ph.D., at least in the so called "hard sciences" (chemistry, geology, physics, biology, mathematics, and the various fields of engineering), is sought after by industry and academia. Professional magazines and *The Chronicle of Higher Education*, the weekly trade paper of academic administrators, are brimming with advertisements for academic positions as well as research jobs in industry. When the young Ph.D. looks for a teaching position, his or her interest is finding a place where the opportunities for getting research funding are best. This means that the laboratories are state-of-the-art, while the actual teaching load is mild, allowing time for research, also, there is a fine library, there are excellent computing facilities, adequate funds for professional travel, and a generally supportive atmosphere for research among senior faculty and administrators. Note that no great emphasis is given to undergraduate teaching in this scheme.

Why is this so? Because of the subtle but forceful and unwritten rule of "publish or perish." The young assistant professor must concentrate on getting tenure in four or five years. Tenure means a guaranteed lifetime job at the institution. To get through the tenure committee, one better have some outside research funding, preferably from a federal source, preferably the National Science Foundation (NSF), NASA, NIH or the Department of Defense. Such funding allows a measure of independence as it contains one's own graduate research assistants, summer salary, travel money and research equipment grants. Heady stuff. Once such funding is secured, research reports will turn into scientific papers presented at international conferences, and turn often into articles in professional journals. This brings about personal contacts at other institutions, scientific reputation among peers, and potential cracks at better positions at more reputable schools. Of course, the person's undergraduate teaching better be acceptable because a lousy student evaluation could trip up the career of people with the most shiny academic pedigrees. However, at the time of tenure one better be able to show a resume with classy looking publications, and impressive outside research funding. Otherwise the tenure committee will decide not to burden the department for the next twenty-some years with an academic dud, regardless of glowing student evaluations in those undergraduate courses. One can always find a visiting professor, a local professional acting as an "adjunct professor" or a graduate teaching assistant to cover those courses temporarily. If the tenure candidate's research doesn't cut it, better we "get rid of him while we can."

There is an immense number of scientific journals on the shelves of university libraries. More are published every month. They are crammed with articles written by professors. In some arcane fields the publications appearing yearly far exceed the capacity of its practitioners to keep up with all the new stuff. Most of these articles are scientifically worthless. Many of them are repetitive. Once a paper is published, there is a great temptation for its author to change a few paragraphs here and there and resubmit it for publication elsewhere. The number of "refereed" publications—those that were reviewed by expert critics before publication—is a critically important part of one's resume. In the field of chemistry, a very intelligent way of screening out worthless publications is used: counting "citations." The more somebody's article was quoted or referred to by other researchers in subsequent publications in the field, the more valuable it is considered.

In academia, writing an undergraduate textbook is not deemed worthy in the eyes of one's academic peers. This is another subtle indication of the fact that teaching, at least undergraduate teaching, is not all that important for the professors.

Doctoral candidates in the hard sciences and engineering have tremendous opportunities for jobs at industrial corporations' research divisions, governmental research organizations, start-up corporations in high-tech areas and other research universities. According to an unwritten rule, graduates do not generally stay on at the university where they obtained their degree. This is to avoid intellectual "incest." At least for a few years, they are advised to go on and work elsewhere. But outside of that, employment opportunities are quite limitless. Teaching positions are only a small portion of these opportunities. This is one of the reasons that Ph. D.s in hard sciences do not prepare themselves for teaching undergraduates. However, having spent as much as ten years in universities, they have enough personal experience about the learning process to be able to handle a teaching job.

It is pertinent at this point to mention that American universities are producing more doctoral degrees in some disciplines than there are jobs for these graduates. Numbers of new doctoral degrees in hard sciences have fallen in recent years, but those in "soft sciences" have grown precipitously. Some universities are adjusting their enrollment accordingly. At some schools, graduate assistantships granted to scientists and engineers are 30 to 40 percent higher than those granted to sociologists, historians, or students in Romance languages. The latter type of graduates may find teaching jobs at smaller colleges, but some can find only part time jobs. Meanwhile industry is clamoring to find computer science and other specialists from foreign countries like India and Israel. There is a tremendous demand for engineers and scientists in America, a need which is definitely not met by our bloated university system. As former Citicorp chairman Walter Wriston wrote in 1992:

"At least 80 percent of all the scientists who ever lived are now alive. In our country at least half of all scientific research done since the United States was founded has been conducted in the last decade. With the total stock of our knowledge doubling about every ten or twelve years, it is clear that our intellectual capital is being formed far more rapidly than tangible capital." [2]

About thirty years ago, Jacques Barzun, historian and highly regarded dean of Columbia University at the time eloquently expressed his criticism:

"Men having found, thanks to the efforts of scientists to discover and of historians to preserve or organize, that inquiry yields useful knowledge, search (or, as it is often truly called, re-search) has become an institution, one of the most massive constituents of Intellect. The name of research has changed from a simple description to a term of honor, and the occupation itself has acquired an inherent sanctity; the quality of the work and its results are secondary. This is shown by the fantastic estimate placed upon research in our seats of learning. To do research is deemed nobler than to teach; the men whose names bring prestige to a university are those whose research has impressed others of equal "research potential". For, I repeat, it is not deemed necessary to discover if only one "produces", production being defined as publication. To bring new and valuable knowledge by lecturing before fifty or a hundred students a year is not research, for it is not publication, except in the legal sense. But to print this knowledge in a periodical where only a few will peer at it with skepticism or dismay that is to enlarge human horizons, to make the university shine with a new glory, and to justify an early promotion.

"Since this reward and those linked with research grants (travel, secretarial help, and freedom from teaching) combine lucre with glory, it is not surprising that inside the university and on its in-

2   Walter B. Wriston: *The Twilight of Sovereignty*, New York: Charles Schribner's Sons, 1992.

dustrial and other fringes the practice or pretense of research should have become a compulsion. Thousands of young men are at work on little papers; thousands more are racking their brains to think of an experiment or study. Most of them worry more about the acceptability of the subject in academic eyes than about their chances of doing and saying something useful, that is, few care about the fitness of the matter and none about the readability of the results. "Communication" occurs by good luck, while everybody groans ritually at the bad writing, excessive length, and prevailing insignificance of what the journals print. In a word, this army of researchers by conviction or impressment are technically pedants.

"But let us be careful. These men may also include the scholars and scientists whose results are original and great, and who add to knowledge while assuring its continuity and discipline. It is the cult and the needless stimulation of research that are pedantic and blamable, whether judged intellectually or economically. And indeed socially, the constraint to do research is blamable as an infringement on the free exercise of one's talents, which may be genuine though not allied to the temperament of the writer of monographs. It seems odd that a profession whose exercise requires the making of fine distinctions should fail to make one between significant knowledge and insignificant scribbling, while insisting pedantically on one restricted means of imparting newfound truth.

"'Significance' itself requires apt and not pedantic interpretation. It does not mean that a searcher after truth should discard all findings for which he cannot at once see the use and meaning. Many discoveries have come from a later study of data amassed without a thesis. A great example is that of Tycho Brahe's observations of the planets, which enabled Kepler to enunciate the laws of orbital motion. Observation may precede hypothesis and be justified. Pedantry results rather from intellectual activity which lacks any intrinsic interest ... but disregards meaning, understanding, interpretation.

"The pedant is really not looking at the object, but going through the motions or technique he has learned. At bottom he is thinking about himself and the relation of his results to himself 'What a good boy am I!' Pedantry is affectation and pretense. The pedant uses knowledge to fashion himself a poultice against the world, to show off virtuosity, to remind himself and others of his industry and skill, and to ogle the reward for sitting in libraries when he might have been sitting in bars.

"The general form of contemporary pedantry derives from natural science. It was about a hundred years ago that scientists began to wage war on philosophers and theologians with the aid of two words which were in fact claims to an exclusive righteousness. Those two words are: 'patient' and 'careful.' When science had justly risen to high estate, the idea that none but scientists exercised patience and care defined the pose of the man of learning. From equating science with the patient accumulation and careful verification of facts, we have come to believe that these props of scientific method suffice for attaining all desired knowledge. Fact-gathering is the one industry that knows no recession, and the stance and speech of science are everywhere imitated. Its serious, numerical look inspires worship and causes despair. Whenever subject matter precludes number, a special language, marked by abstraction and heroic detachment, must be devised to prove oneself justified in spirit and one's words worthy of credence." [3]

The first American Ph. D. Degree was awarded in the middle of the nineteenth century (Yale, 1861) to a mechanical engineer doing research to improve gas turbines. Some 140 years later, in the light of the explosive growth in knowledge, there is no end to valuable doctoral research topics in

3   Jacques Barzun: *The House of Intellect*, New York: Harper, 1959.

the scientific and engineering areas. The federal government alone spent $ 34 billion on scientific research in 1999. Overall research and development expenditures in America in the same year is estimated at $ 247 billion. There is plenty of work to do in the "hard" sciences.

The so called "soft sciences," history, economics, linguistics, psychology, English, geography and the others follow the lead of (or perhaps ape) the "hard" fields, if not in spirit but certainly in the degree of pedantry. They insist on original "research" too. For this purpose they amass heaps of data and subject it to statistical analysis leading sometimes to dubious conclusions wrapped in jargon. Alternatively, they may locate some new information in dusty attics or archives. Writing a new biography of a minor eighteenth century poet will qualify for a doctoral dissertation. In humanistic disciplines the good topics have long been "searched and re-searched out." Most current doctoral "research" involves insignificant minutiae about worthless and often dull topics. The degree of irrelevance of some of the subjects studied by future liberal arts professors would astound uninitiated observers. The January, 1999 meeting of the American Historical Association in Washington, D.C., participants were treated to scientific papers on the history of the deaf and the assorted sufferings of women, ethnic minorities and the poor. Papers entitled "Violence against Polish Female Bodies and Identity during World War II" and "Saints at the Gate: Women who Defied Barbarians and Saved Christian Civilization" makes one wonder why one should to take a course from a history professor who honed his skills on abstruse topics like these.

The problem is that there is little demand for these newly minted doctorates in the marketplace. Industry may need people who are literate and would make good assistant marketing managers, but this is considered an unworthy position for a person holding a doctorate in the social sciences. The real possibility for employment is in the academic world where jobs are scarce. The lucky ones find teaching positions and spend their lives on academically replicating themselves. Not being appreciated by the world outside academia, many doctoral graduates of the "soft" sciences often become embittered idealists. This sometimes leads them toward exhibiting Leftist tendencies and espousing "political correctness," code for aggressive ultra-left political indoctrination of students.

Faculty members doing worthwhile research maintain their contact with the cutting edge of their field. This allows them to be much better teachers than those colleagues who claim that their primary interest is teaching, hence refrain from doing any research. One of the major problems of higher education is that the educators are not required to collect their "continuing education units" in a number of professions. Like the U.S. Congress, they make laws that apply to anyone but themselves. As a result, there are many professors over the land who haven't cracked a book or flipped open a professional journal for ages. The students have no way of knowing this.

Doctoral dissertations accepted by American universities are catalogued, collected and made available to the public by the *UMI Dissertation Abstracts,* now a Bell & Howell company. The advent of the Internet allows anyone to identify and validate the doctoral degree of some 1.4 million people on the website:

http://wwwlib.umi.com/dxweb/

Just by typing in a name, the full citation of the individual's dissertation title, the granting institution, the degree, the year granted and the page count of the dissertation is provided. One may order a printed copy of the dissertation but the title itself often provides plenty of clues to the dissertation's intellectual depth. One can have a great deal of fun looking up the often shabby academic work of many people who insist on being addressed as 'doctor' for the rest of their lives. One example is the Ph.D. dissertation title of the long-time president of a respected Southern university (slightly altered to protect the culprit): "An Inquiry into the Possible Relationship Between the Success of a Social Sorority and its Adherence to Sound Business Principles and Practices." This 35-year-old hog wash qualifies him to be reverently addressed as "Doctor."

Under the collegiality and mutual polite academic respect there are rancorous fights between faculty members, academic units, departments and colleges for scarce resources. On the top of these discords, there are subtle antagonisms based on real or perceived rankings among disciplines. Professors of medicine sit next to God. Law professors feel superior to engineers, who, in turn, look down on business management. Business college types scorn the psychology department and everybody scoffs at the college of education in which Phys-Ed people are often the lowest on the totem pole.

While within a university all professions claim equality, the range of salaries reflects, to some extent, the "real world" spread of incomes. The table across shows average salaries (assistant through full professors) on standard none (or ten) month contracts in a selection of fields for public and private four year colleges. This information was extracted from a report by the College and University Personnel Association on salaries in the 1997-98 academic year. The spread of these salary ranges is quite startling. In private universities, for instance, the salary of an engineering professor is about 60 percent larger than that of a professor in

ACADEMIC FIELDS	Public Universities $ (9 month contract)	Private Universities $ (9 mo. contract)
Engineering	67,918	71,011
Physical Sciences	62,956	65,710
Accounting	63,947	60,059
Anthropology	53,648	54,544
Psychology	53,091	49,925
Mathematics	52,673	51,261
Education	50,024	45,182
Fine Arts & Art Studies	48,349	44,937
Teacher Education	47,353	42,832

Average Faculty Salaries, 1997-98

teacher education. This compares to 'real life' situations quite well. A practicing engineer in industry could command over twice the salary of a high-school teacher. One must keep it in mind that these salaries are for nine months. Professors have a chance to collect almost an additional third of their income through research and consulting in the summer.

Although the trend may be reversing, another interesting statistic from the same source is that, overall, professors in four-year public universities make higher salaries than their equivalents in non-profit private universities, $ 53,296 versus $ 51,448. If one considers each university's benefit package added to the base salaries, the difference is even larger. A notable exception is the engineering professors' salaries in private institutions. The reason is that engineering is an expensive discipline to set up and operate: hence most private schools can't afford it. Those who can — like MIT and Caltech — have the finest engineering schools of the country where the best professors teach, pulling down very respectable salaries in addition to their stellar consulting fees from the cream of our nation's industry. They more than deserve it. Smaller private schools, if they have engineering programs at all, often have poorly equipped laboratories and their professors are paid poorly too.

The figures in the table are averages. The top private universities pay stellar salaries to their full professors.

The highest average salaries in 1998-99 paid to full professors were as follows:

- Rockefeller U. $ 125,400
- Harvard U. $ 122,100
- Stanford U. $ 117,000
- Princeton U. $ 114,900

At larger schools the faculty incomes are generally larger, partly on account of the possibility of summer teaching and/or research, which could add as much as 30 percent to one's yearly base salary. Also, at larger universities one will find the professors who are active in research, and have a respectable list of scholarly publications and plenty of industrial contacts to pick up occasional consulting and wider reputation. They command larger paychecks.

The salary figures shown in the table earlier are averages in the various disciplines. The spread between the salary of a freshly hired assistant professor just out of his doctoral program and a full professor with decades of service could be quite large. The professor may earn twice the salary of the new hire, or more. In setting salaries and yearly raises this often causes problems. Every one wants a raise, most want an above average raise. The expensive full professor's above average raise may wipe out even an average raise for several young assistant professors. Distributing a set amount of money for yearly raises cause a great deal of anguish in an academic department, both for the chairman and the faculty members.

Also, there is a great deal of competition among universities for the finest recent doctoral graduates from the best schools. The applicants demand salaries that are often out of line with the current salary range in a particular department. Bringing in a new assistant professor with a salary, say, 20 percent higher than comparable people already in house causes lots of headaches. Losing the best faculty candidates on account of inadequate salary offers puts the future of a department in a dim light.

In economically hard-stressed states it is difficult to convince the state legislature that professorial salaries need to be competitive. Richer states can use increased salaries and benefits to lure the best professors away from poorer ones. According to data from the U.S. Department of Education, the five highest nine or ten month contracts of average full professors in the 1997-98 academic year were as follows:

- New Jersey - $ 90,537
- Connecticut - $ 88,039
- Delaware   - $ 85,429
- California   - $ 82,837
- Pennsylvania - $ 81,634

The five worst paying states were:

- West Virginia - $ 58,914
- Wyoming   - $ 58,437

- Idaho - $ 54,788
- North Dakota - $ 52,267
- South Dakota - $ 49,954

Obviously, state universities where the salaries are generally low will tend to lose their best professors to better paying states, unless they happen to be fly-fishing enthusiasts or lovers of wide open spaces. Even if the difference in the cost of living is taken into account, looking at the huge salary differences the cost of these desires will be considered way too high. Consequently, richer states tend to have better state universities.

Among professors of small colleges, two-year programs and colleges of education, the Doctor of Education, or Ed. D. degrees are prevalent. A doctorate in education does not involve real research. One can not use pupils as guinea pigs, thank God. The dissertation usually involves some statistical work of educational nature, often of dubious value, comparing one set of data to another to prove an often trivial point.

Ed.D. degrees are granted at colleges of education. In Europe, high school teachers are university graduates, chemists, mathematicians, historians, etc. who, along with their academic diplomas, obtain teaching certificates. In America a Nobel Prize in mathematics would not qualify a person for a teaching job at a public school. Instead, students go to a teachers' college, take some mathematics courses (not too many, though) along with a whole bunch of courses on how to teach, on the history of American education and stuff like that. Education students do not take courses like statistics and child psychology from the mathematics and psychology departments: history tells us that they may not be able to pass them. Hence the teachers' college offers its own watered-down courses: educational statistics, child development, etc..

Educational jargon is a bane in academia. The extent of its use is inversely related to the difficulty of the subject matter. Jargon gets thicker as the substance of the related information gets thinner. In education circles, for example, one hears the word "dichotomy" very often. It refers to two, usually contradictory, opinions on a given matter. Although it indicates an erudite mind, the true meaning in plain English is that the speaker has really no clue about the matter one way or another. It gets worse: educational statistics reports published by the U.S. Department of Education sometimes contain the word "trichotomy." It means that the writer is totally lost.

Education doctorates are earned, on the average, at the age of 44, compared to about age 32 in other fields. There are two causes for this. One is that once a young elementary or high school teacher is tenured in a school district, say at the age of 24, the only sure way to increasing her income significantly is by obtaining advanced degrees. For the professors of teachers' colleges who are generally paid for a nine-month teaching schedule, additional income for summer teaching is most desirable, so the education establishment encourages the state government to "improve" teacher preparation by insisting on continuing education during summers, when they are not working anyway. This generates summer pay for the professors. If the summer work is nothing but loosely supervised "practice teaching", so much the better. Everybody gains.

SAT average scores by expected college majors in 1994's freshmen students ranged from 788 for home economics students to 1082 for mathematics majors. Engineering was third from the top with an average score of 999. Education was third from the bottom with 854. Given the well established fact that education students, with few exceptions, come from the lower half of the student body in ability, and adding to it that the education faculty also comes from the same intellectual pool, the results for America's educational scene are devastating.

Before going any further, we should take a look at the current quality of teaching. Its best measure is the grades students receive. According to a 1969 report[4] 48 percent of students reported a cumulative grade point average of C+ and lower, and only 7 percent at A- or above. By 1993, these numbers had changed to 21 and 26 percent, respectively. Either we have experienced a rapid growth of diligence and intelligence among our youth in the past 30 years, a very unlikely scenario, or our professors are mollycoddling the students. Interestingly, students of the college of education end up as valedictorians at many universities; they get all the good grades.

There is a special group of college professors to be found at small schools and two year colleges. They are the self-styled "scientists" with an Ed. D. degree who have taken a dribbling of courses in geology, biology and the like. With such scanty scientific backgrounds, they declare themselves "environmentalists", for example, or other ill-defined but impressive-sounding experts. Although their scientific background is minimal, with their "doctorate"

4   Arthur L. Levine and Jeanette S. Cureton: *When Hope and Fear Collide: A Portrait of Today's College Student*, San Francisco: Jossey Bass, 1998.

they have the potential to dazzle their sophomoric students. They even show up as scientific expert witnesses at court trials. Since there is no national professional accreditation at the graduate level, people get away with these fake degrees. Charlatanism is alive and well at quite a few American colleges.

Academics are ever conscious of their rank and privileges. Under most state laws, a professorial contract is more like that of a contractor than an employee. The university cannot spell out the office hours of a professor or the way he or she is to perform between 8:00 AM and 5:00 PM. As long as the professor meets his scheduled classes with some regularity and provides office hours for his students, he can do with his time as he pleases.

Professorial snobbery is another interesting item. At big, doctoral level schools, the proper way to address a professor is to call them just that: "Professor." Not "Doctor." The point is that anybody can be a doctor, but few are professors. After all, professors train the Doctors. But if one walks into a small college, the professors are to be called Doctor. At a small college, if someone is referred to as Professor, it is likely that he or she doesn't have a doctorate. Big difference!

In the classroom the student may be exposed to teachers of various ranks. The lowest rank is that of a teaching assistant, the TA. These are graduate students who get an assistantship that pays a rather low wage and comes with a tuition waiver. In return for these benefits the graduate student teaches one or two undergraduate courses under a minimal supervision by a professor. In spite of the negative publicity one reads in the papers, most teaching assistants do a very creditable job of teaching and they interact well with their students who are not much younger than they are.

Instructors rank higher than teaching assistants, although quite often they are also working on their advanced degrees. They are often part timers, or full-time university employees without the necessary qualifications for a tenure track teaching position, yet experienced in some area, such as conducting laboratory instruction. Often instructorships are offered to people with family obligations who would not be able to make do with the low pay of a graduate assistant. The work is the same but the compensation is better.

The lowest tenure track faculty position is that of an Assistant Professor. Often assistant professors are just out of their doctoral work, in full time teaching positions. At the end of, typically, four years, they seek tenure. If they are good, they may get tenure and promotion to Associate Professor at the same time. However, to be promoted from Associate Professor to Professor takes many years. Promotion to "full" professor status is a very political matter in academia. The Promotion Committee of the department has to be impressed by the quality of teaching, the magnitude of research involvement as determined by the number of research dollars brought in, the number of professional articles published, presentations at regional or international symposia, and so on. Behind all this facade, there are the personal dislikes and friendships, professional jealousies and the plain fact that there may be just too many old and established professors in the given specialty and the upper ranks are crowded. Highly qualified associate professors have been known to move to other institutions on account of poor promotional prospects at their home institutions for reasons that have nothing to do with their academic qualifications.

A keen observer of academia, author Charles J. Sykes, summarized his complains about higher education and its practitioners. He wrote:

"A bill of indictment for the professors' crimes against higher education would be lengthy. Here is a partial one:

"They are overpaid, grotesquely underworked, and the architects of academia's vast empires of waste.

"They have abandoned their responsibilities and their students. To the average undergraduate, the professorate is unapproachable, uncommunicative, and unavailable.

"In pursuit of their own interests research, academic politicking, cushier grants they have left the nation's students in the care of an ill-trained, ill-paid, and bitter academic underclass.

"They have distorted university curriculums to accommodate their own narrow and selfish interests rather than the interests of their students.

"They have created a culture in which bad teaching goes unnoticed and unsanctioned and good teaching is penalized.

"They insist that their obligations to research justify their flight from the college classroom despite the fact that fewer than one in ten ever makes any significant contribution to their field. Too many maybe even a vast majority spend their time belaboring tiny slivers of knowledge, utterly without redeeming social value except as items on their resumes.

"They have cloaked their scholarship in stupefying, inscrutable jargon. This conceals the fact that much of what passes for research is trivial and inane.

"In tens of thousands of books and hundreds of thousands of journal articles, they have perverted the system of academic publishing into a scheme that serves only to advance academic careers and bloat libraries with masses of unread, unreadable, and worthless pablum.

"They have twisted the ideals of academic freedom into a system in which they are accountable to no one, while they employ their own rigid methods of thought control to stamp out original thinkers and dissenters.

"In the liberal arts, the professors obsession with trendy theory — which is financially rewarding — has transformed the humanities into models of inhumanity and literature departments into departments of illiteracy.

"In the social sciences, professors have created cults of pseudo-science packed with what one critic calls "sorcerers clad in the paraphernalia of science. . . wooly-minded lost souls yearning for gurus," more concerned with methodology and mindless quantification than with addressing any significant social questions.

"In the sciences, professors have mortgaged the nation's scientific future and its economic competitiveness to their own self-interest by ignoring undergraduates and an epidemic of academic fraud.

"In schools of education, their disdain for teaching and the arrogance with which they treat their students has turned the universities into the home office of educational mediocrity, poisoning the entire educational system from top to bottom.

"They have constructed machinery that so far has frustrated or sabotaged every effort at meaningful reform that might interfere with their boondoggle.

"Finally, it has been the professors relentless drive for advancement that has turned American universities into vast factories of junkthink, the byproduct of academe's endless capacity to take even the richest elements of civilization and disfigure them into an image of itself." [5]

There is not much to add to these truths, except a last statement from Sykes:

"Almost single-handedly, the professors — working steadily and systematically — have destroyed the university as a center of learning and have desolated higher education, which is no longer higher or much of an education."

Sykes is not the only critic. Ronnie Dugger, who wrote an incisive study on the history of the University of Texas stated:

"The university is the conscience of the culture, the most important institution in Western civilization, yet it is failing, and failing in too many ways, in its shattered course system, its dubious and sometimes immoral uses of learning, the political uses of its status and resources, its oppressions of the freedom of the mind, many of its professors becoming researchers, profiteers, and malingerers, its graduates specialized, uneducated, and angry. Serving special interests and special people, the university is becoming a students' orphanage." [6]

5   Op. cit.

6   Ronnie Dugger: *Our Invaded Universities*, New York: Norton, 1974.

7. The Elitist Syndrome

The pinnacles of university education in the Anglo-Saxon world are, without any doubt, Britain's Oxford and Cambridge universities. Established in the beginning of the twelfth century, about 400 years before Harvard, they educated the political and intellectual leaders of England throughout her history. British novelist Len Deighton, a prolific writer of bestsellers, once described them with the following words:

> "Oxford and Cambridge provide an excellent opportunity to learn, although not better than any well-motivated student can find in a first class library. But an Oxbridge education can make graduates feel that they are members of some privileged elite, destined to lead and make decisions that will be inflicted upon lesser beings. Such elitism must of necessity be based on expectations that are often unfulfilled. Thus Oxbridge has not only provided Britain with its most notable politicians and civil servants but its most embittered traitors too."

Harvard University is America's answer to Oxford and Cambridge. Established to train preachers for the Pilgrims as early as 1635, it has a library complex with some 13 million books, graduate programs in just about every academic field, and a legendary reputation for academic excellence. There is no doubt that Harvard is at the top of America's elite institutions. With over 6,600 undergraduates, with some 16,700 applicants each year from which about 2,100 are admitted and 1,652 enrolled — one in ten applicants — it perhaps is the most selective of America's universities. If a student is truly brilliant, wants to go, and is lucky enough to get accepted, he or she will get a superb education. But a graduate of Harvard's undergraduate school and former Rhodes scholar once expressed his regret that he went there. "It is far too competitive, needlessly so," he lamented.

One hundred years ago, one of the admissions requirements at Harvard College was the performance of several of 40 physics experiments under a teacher's supervision. The records of the observations and measurements had to be submitted with the application for admission. These pre-admission tests are now replaced by the SAT scores and a huge dose of politics.

Although Oxford trained embittered traitors, most of them — Kim Philby, Guy Burgess, Donald Maclean and Anthony Blunt, to mention a few — escaped to the Soviet Union. Harvard, apparently, kept its Communists on the faculty. Their influence on Harvard's admissions policy is palpable.

On the matter of leftist political activism in Harvard's admissions policy, buried in the editorial page of the November 16,1998, *Wall Street Journal* was a remarkable essay, which exposes the true and hidden story of who is really "under represented" in our elite schools, and who are the real victims of ethnic bigotry in America. The author is Ron K. Unz, a Harvardian 20 years ago and a Silicon Valley enterpreneur, who led the successful state initiative, Proposition 227, to abolish bilingual education in California.

Today at Harvard College, according to Mr. Unz, Hispanic and black enrollment has reached seven percent and eight percent, respectively, slightly less than the ten percent and twelve percent of the US. population that is Hispanic and black. This has been a cause of protests at Harvard, as Hispanics and African-Americans insisted on more proportional representation.

Unz goes on to report that nearly 20 percent of the Harvard College student body is Asian-American, and 25 percent to 33 percent is Jewish, though Asian-Americans make up only three percent of the US. population and Jewish-Americans even less than three percent. Thus, 50 percent of Harvard's student body is drawn from about five percent of the US. population.

One must keep in mind that even if the undergraduate admission process is *politically correct*, Harvard's fame rests on its magnificent medical school, on its venerable law school and on its stellar graduate school of business which is rolling in money. Professors in these grand graduate and professional programs apparently don't give a hoot how the College is selecting its undergraduates. They do, however, take an exception to the quality of graduates Harvard College produces, who, in turn apply at their graduate schools. As the well known author, professor Martin L. Gross wrote:

"It seems that law school admissions officers ignore magna cum laude and cum laude honors from Harvard as meaningless. *Why? Because Harvard generously handed out honors to an astonishing 84 percent of a recent graduating class!* ... Harvard, the inner sanctum the leader of the New Establishment, is the leader in false praise. There, the *average* grade is now A- to B+." It is to nobody's surprise that an undergraduate degree from Harvard is not necessarily a ticket to somewhere." [1]

Harvard leads the nation's selective, elite colleges, followed by Yale, Princeton, Stanford and quite a number of others. What does this selectiveness really mean? It is essentially an advertising gimmick. High numbers of applicants and low admission percentages, the mere fact of hard to get in, after a few years will establish a college's "quality" as perceived by the general public. As one admissions ana-

---

1   Martin L. Gross: *The End of Sanity*, Avon Books, 1997.

lyst said: "...we are, after all, businessmen in that our business is producing and selling education." [2]

Education expert and prolific author Harlow G. Unger explains:

"most of the same books are available in almost every college library throughout the country. The knowledge is there for any motivated student to obtain and absorb. In other words, you can get almost the same education and achieve the same measure of success regardless of which college or university you attend. It's true that many brilliant and successful people graduate from Yale, Harvard, Princeton and Stanford universities, but equally gifted students also graduate from less-known schools such as City College in New York, Whittier College in California (alma mater of President Nixon) or Eureka College in Illinois (where President Reagan graduated), to mention just a few. What, then, is the difference between various categories of colleges and universities?

"The answer is the difficulty of entrance; the renown of the faculty; the funds and facilities available for education, recreation and living quarters; and the degree of academic commitment demanded of each student and faculty member. The vast majority of the more than 1,500 four-year degree-granting colleges in the United States operate on near or complete open enrollment — i.e., they accept nearly 100 percent of all applicants. There are more than 1,200 colleges that operate in this fashion, accepting students almost on a first-come, first-served basis but giving preference to students from the immediate geographic area. The

2   Charles J. Shields: *The College Guide for
     Parents*, New York: College Entrance
     Examination Board, 1995.

vast majority of publicly operated state colleges and universities fall into this category.

"A recent *Barron's* listed only about 130 American colleges that accept fewer than half their applicants. Only 88 (e.g., Colgate, Emory, Grinnell, Lehigh, Oberlin, Reed, Smith, Villanova, etc.) fell into the "Highly Competitive" category. These colleges generally accepted between one-third and one-half of their applicants."[3]

In a letter to the editor of *The Chronicle of Higher Education* Harvard graduate Gene Schuckman wrote in 1999:

"While an Ivy degree conveys an aura of prestige, intellect, and stature, and presents a series of "intangibles" that are difficult for economists to quantify, the opportunities that are present at "less selective institutions" such as state universities can level the playing field - but only if a student is sufficiently motivated and mature enough to capitalize on those opportunities.

"To the extent that the Ivies select students who already possess greater motivation than their peers, then I would agree that the cost of attending an Ivy is justified. But by no means would I say that attending an Ivy is necessarily the right decision for a student who … might be equally successful at a public institution when such factors as scholarships, honors programs, breadth of curriculum and proximity to family and loved ones are factored into the decision."

A very careful statistical analysis of data based on a large number of college graduates appears to confirm Schuck-

<hr>

3   Harlow G. Unger: *A Student's Guide to College Admissions;* New York: Facts on File, 1995.

man's opinion. Andrew Mellon Foundation's Stacy Dale and Princeton University professor Alan B. Krueger reported that students who attend higher tuition schools earn more after entering the labor market, but students attending more competitive schools have higher average SAT scores. Hence, all other things being equal, students attending a higher average SAT school tend to have a lower rank in class. Dale and Krueger concluded:

"The improvement in class rank for students who choose to attend a less-selective college may help explain why those students do not appear to incur lower earnings; employers (and graduate schools) may value their higher class rank by enough to offset any effect of attending a less selective college on earnings" … "our findings cast some doubt on the view that peer group quality, as measured by the average SAT score of the students who attend a college, is an important determinant of students' subsequent life outcomes." [4]

Nationally syndicated columnist Thomas Sowell[5], himself a magna cum laude graduate of Harvard, agrees:

"Harvard turns out some very smart people because Harvard takes in some very smart people — and it cannot reduce

4   Stacy Berg Dale and Alan B. Krueger: *Estimating the Payoff to Attending a More Selective College: An application of Selection on Observables and Unobservables*, Working Paper # 409, Princeton University, December 1998.

5   Thomas Sowell: Getting your money's worth at college, *Washington Times Weekly Edition*, Dec. 27, 1999.

their intelligence in four years ... Don't waste your hard-earned money on ivy. ... There are very prestigious colleges and universities where your son or daughter can graduate without ever having taken a single course in mathematics, science, English or economics. ... Many colleges are like a cafeteria where you can get either steak and potatoes or junk food. There are usually lots of junk food courses at even the most prestigious — and expensive — colleges and universities."

Trying to get admitted to "the best" college is carried to hysterical extremes by many graduating high school students. They prepare lists ranking the "best schools" according to their admissions statistics, groups of the most desired down to "acceptable." They devise complex application strategies and marshal their resources, letters of recommendation, essays, and extracurricular experiences to impress college admissions officials. Among all these things the purpose of the whole thing, what they really want to learn for a lifetime career, is all but forgotten.

Extremely high tuition is the hallmark of our most selective colleges, even though they all have enormous endowments. For instance in 1998-99 Dartmouth students paid $ 29,340 a year for tuition, room and board. The school's endowment on June 30, 1997 amounted to $ 1.278 billion. This endowment produces enough income that Dartmouth could waive tuition for all students. It did — but only to those whose presence on campus was needed in the interest of social engineering. In 1769, Dartmouth College was chartered to educate Indians. Today, it is 58 percent white. It is safe to assume that few of the remaining 42 percent paid full tuition. In the 1995-96 school year, Dartmouth's president was paid a salary of $ 397,026, amounting to $ 71.45 per student. Even Dartmouth's treasurer received $ 266,794 in 1995-96, the wage for shuffling around all that endowment money. Running a non-profit private school can be big business.

One of the admissions criteria used by the most selective colleges is the SAT. In 1995, for instance, Harvard and Caltech, MIT, Yale and Princeton boasted the highest SAT scores among the elite schools. *USA Today*[6], however, learned that schools count up their students' SAT scores differently. Some do not include their athletes, others use the numbers based on all accepted applicants; others count all enrolled students. Apparently, schools will manipulate their numbers to make themselves look good.

The toughest schools to get into are Harvard, Princeton and Yale. They admit about 14 percent of their applicants. To look at this another way: over 85 percent of superbly qualified applicants who will carry a lifelong memory that they didn't make it. They are in good company: There are well over 20,000 high school seniors who become their schools' valedictorians each year. If they filled the freshman class of each of the eight Ivy League schools, plus Duke, Stanford and the University of Chicago, there would be still about 3,500 to go to the University of Illinois, Michigan, Purdue, UCLA, Georgia Tech, UC Berkeley, and other educational powerhouses. They probably are getting just as good an education as the "lucky ones," and will be just as successful in their careers after graduation. They will also save a considerable amount of money.

6   Pat Ordovensky: *Getting into College,*
Washington, D.C.: Gannett, 1995.

Then again, the really tough schools to get into are Cooper Union in New York and the College of the Ozarks in Missouri. The former admits about 13 percent of its applicants, the latter a mere seven percent. Both are free. Strangely, they are never mentioned as "elite" schools.

One major difference between selective and non-selective schools is the "name." A "name" school, such as Harvard, Yale, Stanford and others, often looks better on a resume to some prospective employer, and that may make it easier to get a job after graduation. It may even help in getting a higher starting salary. In practice, however, the shine rubs off in about six months or so, when performance evaluations are made. It is therefore rather silly to spend in excess of $ 100,000 attending an undergraduate four-year college solely for the school's prestige, its snob appeal.

As the eminent historian Jacques Barzun[7] once wrote:

"The greatest power propelling American universities is Prestige. This is a postwar invention. For prestige must not be confused with reputation or greatness and glory, which existed before. Greatness and a glorious reputation descended on institutions after a long course of remarkable achievements. Prestige is preposterous, i. e., it is acquired first instead of arriving last. Prestige means choosing faculty appointees who will look stunning in the press release. Prestige means getting the man or the line of goods that has just come into prominence. Prestige means picking up the top people in mid-career so that nobody can fail to see their beauty, instead of farsightedly judging the young and future kings. Prestige means image-coddling for maximum visibility.

7   Jacques Barzun: *The American University*, New York: Harper & Row, 1968.

Prestige means getting a good rating in the surveys and polls of excellence, and avoiding trouble so as to appear in the press both frequently and favorably. Prestige, in a word, is commercial advertising."

Dean Barzun quotes a university relations officer: "We had to reorient our image to make it visibler."

The so called "selective" colleges are mostly selective because it is one of their attractions. The entrance requirements of these "dream schools"— at least on the surface — appear to rule out anyone who is not an academic, artistic or athletic hotshot. The admission statistics, the number of applicants compares with the number of those admitted does not give a true picture. These numbers are blurred by considerations of race, other factors such as athletic admissions, geographic factors and several others. What appears to be an admission rate of one in ten, for a well qualified student who is a member of the unprotected majority the true rate is as high as one in 50 or higher.

But all of this is a mirage. Of the over 1.6 million entering freshmen each year fewer than one in 1,000 will enter Harvard. Including all of the "most selective" colleges, those admitted will still be fewer than one in 100. The remaining 99 percent of the entering freshmen will go to other universities. Will the lucky one percent run the country when they get into the "real world?" Most unlikely. As has been amply demonstrated, the real action is mostly at the big state and private universities, not at the erstwhile watering holes of the WASP elite.

8. The Communist Intrusion

There is a dark cloud gathering over liberal arts education at America's most eminent universities. It is the propagation of Marxist-Leninist philosophy and, in some cases, downright Communist radicalism among faculty and administrators. With the Soviet Union gone, and Communist regimes precariously maintained in places like North Korea, Vietnam, Cuba and the Peoples Republic of China, the only remaining Communist propaganda institutions in the Western world are some of America's so-called "elite" universities.

The History Department of Harvard University should get five shimmering red stars as a mark of recognition for its unparalleled infamy in embracing Bolshevism, if what columnist Robert Stacy McCain[1] reported is correct. Here is what he wrote:

"A leading historian of Soviet atrocities contends that Yale University Press 'blackballed' him as an editor of a planned series of works on communism for what his U.S. critics called the 'excessively anti-Bolshevik tone' of his work.'

"Vladimir Brovkin, a researcher and author of three books on the history of the Soviet Union, proposed that a series of books on the Soviet gulag prison camp system would 'explain how and why a monstrous system of mass terror came into being'.

1   'Revisionists close the book on Soviet historian';
     The Washington Times National Weekly Edition,
     1998; reproduced by permission.

"But in August, Yale University Press rejected the proposal when members of an advisory committee charged that Mr. Brovkin's anti- Communist viewpoint would "threaten the scholarly reputation of the entire project.

"Yale's rejection was not the first such experience for Mr. Brovkin, who was an associate professor of history at Harvard University from 1990 until last year.

"I've been told this was one of the reasons they denied tenure to me at Harvard" Mr. Brovkin, now in a temporary teaching position at American University, said of his research into Bolshevik atrocities under Soviet leader Vladimir Lenin. 'It's politically incorrect, they told me.'

"Jonathan Brent, executive editor of Yale University Press, scoffs at Mr. Brovkin's claims. 'This is a tempest in a teapot as far as Yale University Press is concerned.'

"Mr. Brovkin's proposal 'was put through the standard procedure for scholarly publications'. The proposal, he said, was submitted to the advisory committee — whose criticisms have been kept anonymous — and of seven responses 'five were quite negative.'

"Describing Mr. Brovkin's claims as 'complete nonsense,' Mr. Brent said he required 'somebody with standing in the profession' to edit the Soviet gulag series, and the committee's criticisms 'made me feel [Mr. Brovkin] lacked credibility.'

"One critic of Mr. Brovkin's proposal argued that Soviet prisoners were sent to the gulag 'in accordance with the laws of the land.'

"Mr. Brovkin, who spent six months out of work last year after he says 'they threw me out of Harvard,' has been outspoken in criticizing leaders of the pro Soviet 'revisionist' school of Russian history who now 'dominate' the field in U. S. universities, according to Richard Pipes, Harvard professor emeritus and author of *The Unknown Lenin.*

"Revisionists 'monopolize jobs to a very large extent and make it very hard for anyone who holds a different point of view to get a job. [Mr. Brovkin] is a very good example,' Mr. Pipes said.

" 'They claim that he's too passionately anti-Communist and demonizes the Soviet regime,' Mr. Pipes said of Mr. Brovkin's critics. 'I've never seen a respectable historian criticize a German scholar for demonizing Hitler or being too anti-Nazi.'

"Mr. Brovkin said the fact that he spent the first 22 years of his life living under the Soviet system — he emigrated from Russia in 1975 — is held against him.

" 'They said the reason I had those [anti-Communist] views because I was an emigre,' said Mr. Brovkin, who graduated from Leningrad University in 1973, got his master's degree in Russian studies from Georgetown in 1977 and earned his Ph.D. in history at Princeton in 1984.

"New Republic Senior Editor Jacob Heilbrunn publicized the Brovkin controversy earlier this month. Citing pro-Soviet views by University of Chicago professor Sheila Fitzpatrick and University of California-Riverside professor J. Arch Getty, Mr. Heilbrunn argued "the Soviet studies field has been captured by revisionists who dismiss as Cold War humbug the notion that the Soviet Union was a totalitarian country.

"In an interview, Mr. Heilbrunn said Mr. Brovkin's 'academic career has been derailed' because of his anti-Communist views. 'These American revisionists are spouting the same propaganda the Soviet government dispensed from the 1920s onward.' The revisionist school of Russian history arose in the 1960s, at the time of a movement toward 'detente' between the West and the Soviet bloc, Mr. Pipes explained. Revisionists depicted the Russian revolution as *a mass movement* — not a Bolshevik conspiracy, Mr. Pipes said, reflecting 'very much the views of the Soviet government.'

"But the collapse of the Soviet Union in the early 1990s led to the opening of secret Communist archives in Russia, and such scholars as Mr. Brovkin have discovered thousands of documents showing the extent of Soviet atrocities. [2]

"Mr. Brovkin said his research 'showed a very grim side' of the Soviet era that 'didn't fit the point of view of those who wanted to see the Bolsheviks as the good guys, the defenders of the people's revolution.'

This is not exactly how Main Street Americans view what Ronald Reagan called "The Evil Empire" that caused the death of over a 100 million people around the world during the twentieth century. It is said that after wars the winners write the history. In America's left wing "revisionist" history departments, the opposite is true.

Harvard's history department doesn't stand alone in American higher education espousing Communist ideology. Marxist-Leninist and Maoist dogma infiltrated liberal-arts education throughout the land. It is an unvarnished fact that America's colleges are undergoing a cultural and academic revolution. As the former University of Wisconsin Chancellor, long time U. S. Secretary of Health and Human Services, Donna Shalala was quoted as saying, there is "a basic transformation of American higher education in the name of multiculturalism and diversity." In essence, there is the complete reversal of the anti-Communist McCarthyism of

2   Brian Crozier: *The Rise and Fall of the Soviet Empire*, Rocklin, CA: Prima Publishing, 1999.

the 1950s. It is in vogue at our liberal arts colleges today to be fervently against the majority of the American people: anti-white, anti-heterosexual, anti-male, anti-business, anti-family, anti-Christian. In many places the lunatics [or, *mental health services consumers*; to use the politically correct idiom] are running the asylum.

Indeed, universities are under attack today—from the inside. Like cancer, revolutionary forces are eating away democracy from the inside. The pseudo-intellectual revolutionary concepts of today's academic left can easily traced back to the defunct Communist tenets. It was taken up by the 1960s dissenters as an ideology in support of their anti-war movement. Author Dinesh D'Souza explains that

"this revolution is conducted in the name of those who suffer from the effects of Western colonialism in the Third World, as well as race and gender discrimination in America. It is a revolution on behalf of minority victims. Its mission is to put and end to bigoted attitudes which permit perceived social injustice to continue, to rectify past and present inequities, and to advance the interests of the previously disenfranchised. Since the revolutionaries view xenophobia, racism, sexism, and other prejudices to be endemic and culturally sanctioned, their project seeks a fundamental restructuring of American society." [3]

According to a report released in September, 1999[4] surveying 33,785 professors at 378 colleges and universities, 39.6 percent consider themselves liberals, 37.2 middle of the road, 17.6 conservative, 0.4 far right, and 5.2 far left. Reporters for the *Dartmouth Review,* examining voter checklists around Hanover, New Hampshire and surrounding communities, found that professors from economics, English, government, history, philosophy and religion are 79 percent Democrat, 18 percent Independent, and only three percent Republican[5]. Apparently there is no effort to seek diversity of political opinion among Dartmouth's liberal arts professors. Faculty members active in leftist political causes often call themselves "liberals." The dictionary's[6] definition of the word "liberalism"is "Political and social philosophy advocating the freedom of the individual and governmental guarantees of individual rights and civil liberties." In this light, if the leftist professors are *liberal* then Stalin and Hitler were great humanitarians. Plain and simple, they are neo-Communists. The campus liberal today is a Bolshevik without a gun.

Among the faculty of America's liberal arts colleges are many aging teachers who started college during the Vietnam War. Many went to school and stayed on for graduate school with the sole purpose of avoiding the draft — a legal way to avoid going to Vietnam. They organized demonstrations, waved the North Vietnamese flag, and burned their bras, their draft cards, and the stars and stripes. As long as the war was on, they stayed within the safety of ivy-covered walls. These people were not selected for their doctorate programs for their stellar intellectual capacity. Rather, they

3   Dinesh D'Souza: *Illiberal Education: The Politics of Race and Sex on Campus;* The Free Press, 1991.

4   *The American College Teacher,* Higher Education Research Institute, UCLA, 1999.

5   Jeffrey Hart: No Diversity of Ideas on Campus Today, *Washington Times, Weekly Edition,* Aug. 7-13, 2000.

6   *Random House College Dictionary,* Rev. Ed., 1988.

shared the common traits of being treasonous and selfish cowards. In that, they are diametrically opposed to their parents, who belonged to the greatest generation of America.

Most of these professional students were not smart enough to learn something useful. They did not became neurosurgeons, they did not invent microprocessors. Rather they studied faint and elusive academic subjects, creating their own pseudo-disciplines, and organized "teach-ins." Many of these stalwart patriots stayed on in academe because there was little demand in the marketplace for doctorates in peace studies or for experts in Latin American liberation theology. You find them today on many campuses as rumpled old professors teaching bizarre courses. Many make their living teaching obscure, economically unrewarding and publicly unappreciated topics to fill up the undemanding elective schedule of today's liberal arts students.

These people are not only some of today's liberal arts professors; they also inhabit the federal government's highest levels. When the commander-in-chief of our armed forces was a former draft dodger, what else could one expect?

Having spent a lifetime in ivory towers, the neo-Bolsheviks are alienated from average hard-working Americans whom they consider socially and intellectually inferior. Because of their esoteric teaching and research interests they never get in contact with the real world as scientists, engineers or other professionals would. Instead, they created their little pseudo-intellectual microcosms, embracing everything that is opposite to what America stands for. They are the professors who teach Neo-Marxism, profess love and understanding of everything that is deviant from the norm, teach all sorts of weird nonsense from eco-criticism to lesbian studies. They are the purveyors of "political correctness." They are the intolerant neo-Communists who are trying to tear apart the social fabric of the nation just when it is experiencing the greatest prosperity in its history. They are the "multiculturalists" who spend their days "celebrating diversity."

As long as one spouts the concepts of and diversity, opposes the Christian religion, capitalism and freedom of speech, he or she is "politically correct." "Correct" thinking and "correct" speech are strictly enforced on many of our campuses, just like Mao-think was once in Red China. In plain English, it means campus speech codes forced on professors and students, circumscribing what can and can not be said in and outside the classroom. Despite their ostensible purpose of protecting the "feelings" of various "traditionally oppressed" groups, these speech codes are nothing else but the systematic violation of the First Amendment. Diversity of *ideas* is not tolerated on campus today. Unless one mouths the party line, he or she is stamped with the appropriate label: sexist, racist, gay-basher, right-wing — whatever implied threat it takes to shut down the opposition.

Multiculturalism is the exact opposite of racial integration. It is celebrated under the banner of "diversity." It encourages segregation by assuring "former victims of the oppressive racist white regime" their own place in the sun, providing segregated dormitories, "studies" programs such as "Afro-American Studies, "Gay and Lesbian Studies," "Women's Studies," and so on. By the way, to call 52 percent of the population a "minority' takes a lot of gall.

As Martin L. Gross writes in *The End of Sanity*:

"The idiocy of the whole idea of special studies for races, ethnicities and genders should be obvious (where are the

Male Studies Programs?) Since America has over sixty minority groups, shouldn't we, in all fairness, accommodate each group's spectrum? Then why not eliminate all non-ethnic or nonracial-based subjects and spend four years navel-examining each other's supposed differences?."

As Kors and Silverglate describe in their carefully crafted book, *The Shadow University*[7]:

"Universities operate with a humanly impoverished notion of 'diversity', excluding personality, social class, spirituality, taste, and private passions. Anyone who knows undergraduates knows that in matters of personality alone, the diverse manifestations of the affirmation of fear of life are, in fact, much more striking and essential than the categories of race, gender, and sexual orientation by which universities today almost uniquely, and for partisan purposes, distinguish among the lives lived there. Indeed, when colleges do think about affirmation and vulnerability, they do so from the racist and misogynistic notions that ego strength correlates to externalities, and that whites, men, and heterosexuals have it while blacks, women, and gays do not. A white male student who lost a father in Vietnam is deemed strong enough by racial definition to hear a professor to call his late father a 'baby killer', whereas a woman or black must be protected from the punch line of a joke."

The last great barrier faced by American blacks was removed by the 1960s civil rights laws, assuring the end of racial segregation. It did not solve the problems of the

7   Kors, Alan Charles and Harvey A. Silverglate:
     The Shadow University, New York: The Free Press,
     1998.

African-Americans in one sweeping change. The education of poor black kids is still inferior after 30 years. Our public schools are generally lousy, but the public schools in disadvantaged urban areas are truly deplorable. The primary problem is money, but it is not the only problem. Helping to improve the kids' self-image can not be separated from teaching self-discipline and responsibility. Instead of these, black students are assured that "black is beautiful" and are passed on to the next class without assuring that they are qualified. When it comes to college time, only the most brilliant go on to professional programs, the others are steered into "Afro-American Studies" only to find out that it doesn't qualify them for any useful job. Most drop out without completing their degree. There are ample opportunities for valuable college education for every qualified black high-school graduate. They could get degrees in science, engineering and business administration, or any other worthwhile profession. Why the great majority of America's blacks put up with the patronizing attitude of the "politically correct" is hard to comprehend.

America's greatness rests on its European civilization, more precisely the Anglo-American cultural values accepted by all immigrants within a couple of generations, whether they came from Poland, Jordan, Columbia or elsewhere. The unifying "melting pot" created a nation and the capitalist economic system that is the envy of the world.

In liberal arts colleges that were subtly taken over by the neo-Communists, classical authors of Western literature are replaced in the required liberal arts curriculum by works written by women and "people of color," works often of dubious scholarship. Sometimes the work, as in the case of an alleged autobiography of an Andean Indian girl, "Rigoberta Menchu" — a Communist agitator's daydream — is found to be totally fabricated, but only after being on the reading lists of our best universities for well over a decade.

Scholarship is replaced by "feel good" topics. White males are put through "sensitivity training" so that they can commiserate with the hordes of the oppressed and made to feel ashamed for their alleged crimes against the long suffering minority. Like in Mao-land, they are forced to perform self-criticism. In the process, American liberal arts education is trashed.

The majority of of the student population in this country is cowed by a gang of masterfully manipulated minorities. All this while the various groups hate each other far more than they hate the majority. Why the white majority in our colleges accept such treatment is hard to explain. According to the study made by the American Council for Education[8] reviewed in an earlier chapter, the political views of the current generation are quite balanced. 54.8 percent consider themselves middle of the road, with 19.3 percent conservative and 19.2 percent liberal (men tend to be slightly more conservative than women). Only 2.8 percent espouse the far left and 1.5 percent the far right. They are obviously not in agreement with the neo-Communist crowd that dominate the college scene in liberal arts.

Administrators of America's colleges who are in the grip of "political correctness" oppose the idea of integration, pluralism, freedom of ideas and the objective study of foreign cultures and civilizations. The fundamental requirement to

8   *The Chronicle of Higher Education*, Aug. 27,
     1999.

get an administrative job at an American university is "the commitment to cultural diversity." It means quite the opposite of what it appears to mean. In the eyes of the "politically correct" academic administrator students are not individuals. Instead, they are divided into groups. There are [traditional] oppressors and oppressed. The "oppressed" are historically disadvantaged groups that are now under the protection of ultra-left "thought police." Many college presidents and deans are hypocritical cowards. They willingly put up with any one of the arrogant minority activist groups who organize a "sit in" in their offices demanding yet another specious concession. Rather than calling in the police and throwing the off campus permanently, they routinely cave in to any demand.

According to the tenets of diversity, multiculturalism and militant defense of victimhood are "politically correct." Yell out "Shorty!" in a campus hallway and you are subject to disciplinary procedure for practicing "hightism." To show an example of this thinking, a professor at Princeton, according to the *Campus Report* of Accuracy in Academia, pronounced: "it is speciestist to judge that the life of a normal adult member of our species is more valuable than the life of a normal adult mouse." That is a "politically correct" statement, at its best, from an obviously demented professor.

Anyone who utters something that may be considered harassing by a protected minority group could be in serious trouble on a campus. The recent "water-buffalo" story is a fine example: a University of Pennsylvania student, who by his name could be stereotyped as Jewish, was upset by noise made by several persons under his window while he studied in his dormitory room. He allegedly shouted down; "Shut up, you water-buffalo!" He was nearly kicked off campus after the six alleged "water-buffaloes" registered their complaint with the university administration. How the affair unfolded is murky. Apparently the boy heard brassy female voices with a discernible Southern drawl, and he — politically incorrectly — stereotyped them as African-American women. The alleged "water-buffaloes," by being in a single-ethnic, single-gender group without a person of contrasting color among them, most certainly behaved in a politically incorrect manner. Whatever happened, this story made the University of Pennsylvania the laughingstock of America.[9] The university's president, under whose watch this sordid affair happened, soon was rewarded with an important position in the Clinton administration.

Other recent horror stories from America's campuses:

A Christian speaker at Syracuse University was heckled by the lesbian Avengers, a radical campus group, who began kissing each other during the speech. The demonstration finally ended in a Bible burning by leftist students, with no intervention from college officials.

When Communist activist Angela Davis was chosen to speak at the University of Chicago, conservative students who tried to protest her appearance were stopped by college officials.

A professor at Cornell University was disciplined for suggesting homosexuals could be "cured."

9   For details, read Kors and Silverglate, op. cit.

In a five-year span, Emory University hosted 34 liberal speakers, including NOW president Patricia Ireland and former Surgeon General Joycelyn Elders, but only five conservative speakers.

The last remaining Communist ideologues, long gone from the halls of the Kremlin, are the history professors in some of our Ivy League schools. According to the Young America's Foundation there are 10,000 self-described Marxist professors teaching at American universities. They keep supporting the idea of an economic system that has been proven all over the world to be unworkable, inhuman, and downright murderous. It stood against everything America stands for. These alienated crackpots thrive on many of America's best campuses. These academics hate the system they live in and would do their utmost to change it. And—only in America—they are given not only a free pulpit to spread their faith, they are often allowed to control the reins. They teach their Leftist dogma as if it were divine truth. Multiculturalism, diversity, feminist studies, gay studies, collectivist economics and revisionist history all push the same party line. This is—to quote nationally syndicated columnist Don Feder—"virtue is color-coded, masculinity is evil, sex has no moral dimension and Marxism works—gulags, rationing and failed five-year plans notwithstanding."

Teachers' colleges are among the primary disseminators of the new dogma. For instance, some of the teacher education courses at the University of Massachusetts at Amherst are titled as follows: "Social Diversity," "Leadership in Changing Times," "Embracing Diversity," "Diversity and Change," "Oppression and Education," "Introduction to Multicultural Education," "Black Identity," "Classism," "Racism," "Sexism," "Jewish Oppression," "Lesbian,Gay/Bisexual Oppression," "Oppression of the Disabled" and "Erroneous Beliefs." With teachers in our schools indoctrinated with such courses the abysmal performance of America's public schools is not surprising.

There is a slow movement in the positive direction. After almost 20 years on the books, affirmative action rules are being slowly erased under the pressure of the voters who prefer meritocracy in America. The movement is fueled by a deep resentment of the majority of the population who despise discrimination, direct or reverse. This trend did not seem to faze Union College, which initiated a faculty recruitment program in the fall of 1998 restricted to blacks and Hispanics. The administration's argument was that "exposing students to a variety of points of view is an essential part of a liberal-arts education. But it's very difficult to do that without a diversity of backgrounds on the faculty."[10] A Hutu scholar from Rwanda is still sought to teach conflict resolution.

Freedom of speech, the most fundamental intellectual and legal concept of America, is not welcome at many U.S. campuses. Why the overwhelming majority of normal professors put up with this trash on our campuses is a mystery. The grim-faced, humorless, strident neo-Bolsheviks should be laughed off campus. For the prospective student and his or her parents, all this shouldn't really matter. They can easily recognize the malady on campus and vote with their feet. Just ask for a copy of the campus speech code, read it, think about it and apply elsewhere. Maybe, after a while, someone in power will get the message.

10   *The Chronicle of Higher Education*, April 16, 1999.

9. Poison Ivy

Under the perplexing slogan of "celebrating diversity", lib-eral-arts colleges unite a ragtag collection of special interest groups whose only common identifier is that they tradition-ally vote for leftist candidates in American national elec-tions. This diversity celebration does not extend to the rest of the world: the diversity of Kurds, Kosovars, Bosniaks, Chechens, Hutus and Tutsies goes unmentioned. The vir-tual takeover of American college campuses by the ul-tra-left allows the training of an entire generation of American students to be the leftist cadres of the future. What Lenin, Stalin and Mao Tse Tung could not attain in the twentieth century, the flag-burning college thugs of the 1960's expect to accomplish from the inside. This training goes on throughout the land. Indeed, American liberal arts colleges are rife with courses whose content would knock the socks off any normal parent.

There is no better proof of the anti-American, pro-Marx-ist-Leninist nature of America's "elite" colleges than the courses they offer to their students. The "politically cor-rect" courses in vogue today are the neo-Communists at-tempt to poison the minds of our future elite.

This chapter presents a collection of bizarre undergraduate course offerings at 25 of the most selective and elite col-leges in the United States. The course descriptions were compiled by the Young America's Foundation[1]. Under the title, *"Comedy and Tragedy"* the report contains selections from 55 universities. The 25 elite colleges reviewed here are role models for many of the 3,800 or so accredited American colleges. For lack of space only a short sample of the eccentric course descriptions in the college catalogs will be given. Only a few will be quoted in full. Similar courses at other institutions will be mentioned by title only.

The course descriptions selected are sorted into six groups:

- Marxist theory praising the merits of Bolshevik ideology;
- anti-Christian topics including magic and witch-craft;
- environmental activism lacking scientific merit;
- deliberately divisive racial issues;
- militant feminist topics and
- courses extolling sexually deviant behavior.

Classifying the courses was sometimes problematic as they often overlapped in their coverage. Many are anti- Christian, racist and sexually deviant at the same time —in one word—diverse, as in "diversity."

Courses on Marxism are so common on some of America's most ivy-covered campuses that the uninitiated observer would believe that Stalin's minions are in command in Washington D.C., the captains of Wall Street are doing 20-to-life in a reeducation camp on South Dakota's Badlands, Mount Rushmore is re-configured for Marx, Engels, Lenin,

1   *Comedy and Tragedy: College Course Descriptions and What They Tell Us About Higher Education Today; 1998-99; Young America's Foundation: 800 292-9231. It is also available on-line: http://www.yaf.org/pubs/comedy/*

Stalin and Mao Tse Tung, and the Iron Curtain is re-erected along the Rio Grande.

Thank God, Communism is in the trash bin of history, its beliefs are thoroughly discredited, its undescribable crimes and horrors are exposed. The Soviet Union is gone, Eastern Europe is free again and one of the last Stalinist outpost, North Korea, is unable to feed her people after 50 years of Marxist leadership. All of this apparently escaped the attention of the faculty of some academic institutions, where the following courses are offered:

AMHERST COLLEGE **Political Science 61** <u>Taking Marx Seriously</u> - *This seminar will be devoted to a close reading of Marx's text. The main themes we will discuss include Marx's conception of the state and civil society, law and morality, and his critique of alienation, bourgeois freedom, and democracy. We will also examine Marx's theories of historical progress, the genesis of capitalist economic relations, and "human emancipation."*

BROWN UNIVERSITY **Philosophy 40** <u>Marxism</u>

BROWN UNIVERSITY **Philosophy 41** <u>Marxism After Marx</u>

SWARTHMORE COLLEGE **Modern Languages and Literatures 65G** <u>Marxism</u>

VASSAR COLLEGE **Economics 102b** <u>Introduction to Marxian Economics</u> - *Marx's theory of capital accumulation. The relevance of Marx's analysis to contemporary capitalism is explored.*

VASSAR COLLEGE **Political Science 272** <u>Marx and Marxist Thought</u>

SYRACUSE UNIVERSITY **Political Science 372** <u>Marxist Theory</u>

OBERLIN COLLEGE **Politics 239** <u>Marxist Theory</u> - *Study of the work of Marx and leading Marxists. Topics include: alienation; materialist theory of history; critique of capitalism; class structure and conflict; capitalist state; ideology and culture; relationship of theory and practice; Marxist feminism; analytical Marxism; post-modern Marxism.*

STANFORD UNIVERSITY **Economics 220** <u>Marxian Economic Theory</u>

BUCKNELL UNIVERSITY **Economics 358** <u>Marxian Economics</u>

WELLESLEY COLLEGE **Economics 249** <u>Marxist and Post-Marxist Economics</u> - *Study of Marx's analysis and critique of capitalism, and of his vision of socialism. Exploration of contemporary post-Marxist or "radical" economics, including Marxist-feminist, anti-racist, and ecological economics. Study of radical economists' analyses of the collapse of communism in the Soviet Union and Eastern Europe, and of their current proposals for economic restructuring, including market and participatory socialism.*

On behalf of the citizens of Poland, Lithuania, Hungary, Bulgaria and the rest: "Thanks, but no thanks, Wellesley."

DUKE UNIVERSITY **History 165** <u>Working Class in the United States - Perspectives on Marxism and Society.</u>

DUKE UNIVERSITY **Cultural Anthropology 139** <u>Marxism and Society</u>

DUKE UNIVERSITY **History 165** <u>Working Class in the United States - Perspectives on Marxism and Society</u>

UNIVERSITY OF CHICAGO **Cinema and Media Studies 247** <u>Left-Wing Art and Soviet Film Culture of the 1920s</u> - *The course considers Soviet "montage cinema" of the 1920s in the context of*

coeval aesthetic projects in other arts. How did Eisenstein's the-
ory and practice of "intellectual cinema" connect to Fernand
Leger and Vladimir Tatlin? What did Meyerhold's
"biomechanics" mean for filmmakers? Among other figures and
issues, we address Dziga Vertov and Constructivism, German
Expressionism and Aleksandr Dovzhenko, and Formalist poetics
and FEKS directors.

Recent surveys on entering freshmen at the nation's colleges indicate that an overwhelming majority are religious.
Catholics, Protestants, Southern Baptists or Methodists,
practicing or not, almost all Americans identify with the
Christian religion. In the year 2000, 84 percent Americans
surveyed claimed to be Christian. Americans lean over
backwards to constantly reassure the sensibilities of minor,
non-Christian religious communities. Politicians talk about
Judeo-Christian values. The U. S. Army appoints Moslem
clerics as chaplains. But the truth is that America is an over-
whelmingly Christian country. One wouldn't know it by
looking at the following academic offerings:

UNIVERSITY OF PENNSYLVANIA **Religious Studies 530**
<u>The Feminist Critique of Christianity</u>

How about a Christian critique of feminism for once?

HARVARD UNIVERSITY **Religion 1416** <u>Feminist Biblical In-</u>
<u>terpretation</u>

VASSAR COLLEGE **Religion 227b** <u>The New Testament and</u>
<u>Early Christianity</u> - *The Christian Scriptures speak with many*
different voices. Some advocate peace, some rebellion; some
praise duty, others a radical rejection of family and all it repre-
sents. What was the earliest Christian message, and how did it
evolve? How do the texts of the New Testament both reflect and
shape the developing Christian communities? This course exam-
ines these unique texts and relates them to the religious, cultural,

and intellectual realities found by individuals and groups in the Mediterranean world from the first century B.C.E. through the third century C.E.

Particularly interesting to note the use of B.C.E. and C.E., for "Before Common Era" and "Common Era" instead of B.C. and A.D., "Before Christ" and "Ante Diem", which was the accepted form of expression throughout the history of Western civilization. With a contemptible pseudo-intellectual arrogance, the distinction sets the tone for the course ostensibly taught as "Religion."

EMORY UNIVERSITY **African American Studies 270M** <u>Religion and Prejudice Reduction</u> - *This theory/practice course uses a "prejudice reduction" approach to address the interaction between religion and social oppression. Why are religions sometimes the cure for persecution and scapegoating, but all too often the cause? To answer that question we will correlate a scapegoat theory of religion (Rene Girard) with a prejudice reduction practicum (Cherie Brown). This strategy will provide us rich resources for critical analysis on the one hand, and also an experiential, interactive process of community building within and beyond the context of the classroom.*

UNIVERSITY OF PENNSYLVANIA **Afro-American Studies 159** <u>The Historical Origins of Racism: Views of Blacks in Early Judaism, Christianity and Islam</u> - *The course examines views and attitudes toward black-Africans as found in the ancient and medieval sources of Judaism, Christianity, and Islam. We will attempt to discover the relationship between these views and racism in Western civilization.*

The Christian churches in America have, traditionally, been the single most powerful force of mutual support among African-Americans. Martin Luther King, Jesse Jackson and countless other black leaders were men of the cloth. Now the academic neo-Communists attempt to destroy this trust by referring to "ancient and medieval sources".

PRINCETON UNIVERSITY **Religion 366** Religion and Sexuality: The Problem of the Erotic - *Religion has traditionally been linked to prominent sexual attitudes—even when it seems most prohibitive, and even in social contexts where the matter of sexuality is not explicitly addressed. We will examine Greek and Roman background to this vast topic—to ask whether arguments for sexual renunciation, arguments against same-sex sexuality, etc., have non-biblical and/or non-revelatory roots far different from the Protestant ones that are normally presupposed.*

SYRACUSE UNIVERSITY **Anthropology 373** Magic and Religion - *Cross-cultural study of magical and religious behavior, ritual, and belief systems in simple and complex societies. Specialists and their craft: shamans, priests. Curing, possession, witchcraft. Millennial and counterculture movements. Religious ideologies and innovations.*

UNIVERSITY OF PENNSYLVANIA **History 025** Western Science. Magic and Religion. 1600 to the Present - *The Western world once had its share of witches, alchemists, astrologers and magicians. They are thin on the ground these days, only to be replaced by New Age or cult-like movements. This course examines magic as it once was, explores the rise of science in the seventeenth and eighteenth centuries, looks at Mesmerism and thesosophy within the framework of radical political movements culminating in the rise of Fascism, and for twentieth century America explores the nature of post-War Big Science and various anti-science movements.*

REED COLLEGE **Anthropology 365** Systems of Magic

HARVARD UNIVERSITY **Folklore and Mythology 108** Witchcraft

HARVARD UNIVERSITY **Folklore and Mythology 109** <u>Shamanism</u>

UNIVERSITY OF PENNSYLVANIA **Women 's Studies 226** <u>Vampires: The Undead</u> - *We will explore the persistence and resilience of vampires in literature and film of the past two hundred years, emphasizing their metaphoric deftness and adaptability as cultural couriers. We shall examine work by Polidori, LeFanu, Stoker, King and Rice and films such as Dracula, Nosferatu, Blood & Roses, Night of the Living Dead, and The Hunger.*

WILLIAMS COLLEGE **Anthropology 331** <u>Witchcraft, Sorcery, and Magic</u> - *Beliefs in magic, malign and otherwise, have been nearly universal in human experience. This course examines these beliefs to understand their cognitive basis, symbolic effectiveness, and social consequences. In particular we will approach the question of "magical thinking": is magical thought "mistaken science" or a universal non-rational way of seeing the world? What does the fact of presumably rational people holding apparently irrational beliefs say about the whole idea of rationality? Are witches self-aware agents who believe in the malign magic they practice, or are they innocent, marginalized victims of hegemonic powers? To answer these and other questions we will draw on case studies from a broad range of ethnographic and historic sources, including Aguaruna love magic, Azande oracles, Voodoo in Brooklyn, and witches in Renaissance Italy and 20th-century England.*

WELLESLEY COLLEGE **Anthropology 236** <u>Witchcraft, Magic, and Ritual: Theory and Practice</u>

The wide range of courses teaching occultism, including voodoo and other magic stuff, inescapably has filtered into our public schools. According to an Associated Press report in March 1999, Catholic parents in White Plains, NY, went to court to stop the Bedford Central School District to promote "Satanism and occultism, pagan religions and New

Age spirituality" and violate the freedom of religion. They won their case.

UNIVERSITY OF CHICAGO **General Studies In The Humanities 278/3 78** <u>The Slavic Vampire</u>

EMORY UNIVERSITY **African Studies 190** <u>Witchcraft, Witch-hunts and Society</u> - *This course will examine and compare the origins and development of witchcraft beliefs and accusations and their relationship to patterns of social, economic and intellectual change in three historical settings: early modern Europe, colonial America, and colonial Africa. It will employ the history of witch hunts to examine how societies have defined and redefined themselves at various points in history, but defining groups of people as "deviant" and as threats to society. The history of witchcraft beliefs and accusations also provides insights into the development of gender relations in society, the history of science, and the development of legal systems. Finally, the course will employ insights gained from the study of witchcraft to examine the history of more contemporary witch hunts, including the persecution of Jews in Nazi Germany and the rise of anti-Communism in the United States in the 1950s.*

Only people with a warped understanding of history can equate the Holocaust and American anti-Communism during the height of the Cold War.

Founded by the Methodists in 1836, today Emory University's student body is 30 percent Jewish. Unabashedly liberal politically, it is one of the finest private universities in the Southeastern United States. It boast an excellent school of medicine, noted for its research. It also houses the Carter Center and a bunch of ultra-Leftist professors.

CARNEGIE MELLON UNIVERSITY **History 79-295** <u>Witchcraft and Dissent in the Middle Ages</u> - *In the late medieval and early modern periods, Christian society in Europe felt itself* *threatened on all sides. Everywhere witches, heretics and dissidents were challenging the established traditions. It responded to these threats by the creation of the Inquisition and other repressive measures. This course surveys the different types of social and religious protests which developed in the medieval and early modern periods, and the means by which established society sought to cope with them.*

BUCKNELL UNIVERSITY **Anthropology 227** <u>Witchcraft and Politics</u>

Few areas of scientific inquiry have been subjected to so much pseudo-scientific pontificating than our environment. Politicians, many of them lawyers with no training in environmental engineering, biology, geology, chemistry or related fields of science whatsoever, have burst upon the political scene in Washington as a warriors for the environment. A common favorite is Global Warming. Even though enormous amount of scientific research was directed to discern a trend of the temperature variations of the Earth caused by human activity, no atmospheric scientist has been able to promulgate a scientifically sound theory that would support the idea. From geologic and other scientific data we know that there have been relatively warm periods followed by cool periods in the past. That the activities of mankind have even the faintest influence on the overall atmospheric conditions of the Earth has not been proven. One wouldn't know this from the following college courses:

DARTMOUTH COLLEGE **Environmental Studies 12** <u>Global Warming, Energy, and the Environment</u> - *This course introduces students to the issues surrounding global warming and the role of energy resources in the United States and world societies. It will examine the scientific basis for environmental and social concerns for present energy resources, including global warming, toxic emissions and wastes, and nuclear proliferation. The relationships between economic, social, environmental, and geo-*

graphic factors in development and exploitation of energy resources and role of public policy will be considered. Particular attention will be given to the scientific basis for renewable and nonrenewable energy resources, energy efficiency, and conservation.

DARTMOUTH COLLEGE **Environmental Studies 73** <u>Environmental Journalism</u> - *This course attempts to teach students how to write clear and interesting articles for the general public on complex, environmental issues. It is an advanced writing seminar, with frequent critiques and rewrites, and with the goal that each student will actually publish an article in a commercial newspaper or magazine.*

Understanding environmental engineering doesn't appear to be a necessary prerequisite for writing on "complex environmental issues." Proselytizing environmental junk science appears to be the aim. The political tilt of the environmental movement is well demonstrated by the fact that Earth Day 'happens' to be celebrated on the birthday of Lenin.

Dartmouth's Board decided in the winter of 1999 to make its 25 fraternities and sororities coeducational. Common sense as well as anti-discrimination laws passed in the 1960s exempt fraternities and sororities from sex-discrimination charges. But the "liberals" march on.

Paul Craig Roberts of the Cato Institute reported[2] :

<hr>

2   *The Washington Times, National Edition, April 12 - 18, 1999.*

"our college curriculums have many voices of hate busy at work preparing a future holocaust, but a voice of Christian love is considered too divisive to be tolerated. Dartmouth College prohibited copies of C. S. Lewis' *Mere Christianity* from being distributed as gifts to students. A dean ruled the book could be considered offensive. Hate has such a hold that love dare not be mentioned".

Dartmouth's Department of Electrical Engineering is world famous, particularly in computer security technology studies. The engineering professors must be very embarrassed on account of their liberal-arts peers.

MIDDLEBURY COLLEGE **Environmental Studies 305** Environmental Policy Practice - *This course is an independent study program based on work at the Sierra Club's Northeast Regional Office in Saratoga Springs, New York. The course is designed to give the student practical experience in the workings of the environmental policy process. A substantial research paper based on the student's experience at the Sierra Club is required. This course must be taken in conjunction with ES 306. Note: Residence in Saratoga is expected. Students may register for two additional courses at Skidmore College in order to earn three or four credits for the semester.*

The fundamental presumption in this course is that the Sierra Club has the ultimate truth on environmental issues. Hug the trees, property rights be damned.

MIDDLEBURY COLLEGE **Religion 295** Faith, Freedom, and Ecology - *This course will introduce students to some of the prevailing questions in environmental ethics, ecotheology, and the emerging field of ecocriticism. What is the proper relationship between humans, the natural world, and the divine? What is our moral responsibility to ourselves and to the planet? How do freedom and constraint play a role in our choices? Do men and women experience nature (and responsibilities toward nature) differently? Lectures and readings will approach these questions* *from a variety of philosophical, historical and religious perspectives (primarily Western) and will include Jewish, Christian, feminist, pragmatist, scientific and Native American voices.*

UNIVERSITY OF CHICAGO **Environmental Studies 134** <u>Global Warming: Understanding the Forecast</u> - *This course presents the science behind the forecast of global warming to enable the student to evaluate the likelihood and potential severity of anthropogenic climate change in the coming centuries. It includes an overview of the physics of the greenhouse effect, including comparisons with Venus and Mars; an overview of the carbon cycle in its role as a global thermostat; predictions and reliability of climate model forecasts of the greenhouse world; and an examination of the records of recent and past climates, such as the glacial world and Eocene and Oligocene warm periods.*

PRINCETON UNIVERSITY **Economics 319** <u>Environmental Economics</u>

CARNEGIE MELLON UNIVERSITY **History 79-111** <u>Cultural and Cross-Cultural Perspectives on Environment</u>

VASSAR COLLEGE **Environmental Studies 150b** <u>Earth System Science and Environmental Justice</u> - *Exploration of the roles that race, gender, and class play in contemporary environmental issues and the geology that underlies them. Examination of the power of governments, corporations, and science to influence the physical and human environment. We will critique the traditional environmental movement, study cases of environmental racism, and appreciate how basic geological knowledge can assist communities in creating healthful surroundings. Examples will come from urban and rural settings in the United States and abroad and will be informed by feminist analysis.*

From 1861 Vassar was a well respected women's college, until it turned coed in the 1960's. From the previous course description one can see that the feminist ambience is alive and well. Go there and you "will be informed by feminist analysis."

OBERLIN COLLEGE **Politics 237** <u>Green Political Theory</u> - *An examination of various political theories in relation to natural environment. Such issues as the exploitation and transformation of nature, the "tragedy of the commons," the social construction of nature, and the development of a "green" political theory and practice will be considered. Readings will be drawn from ancient and early modern political theory as well as from sources in neo-Malthusianism, ecosocialism, social ecology, deep ecology, ecofeminism, postmodernism, and liberal approaches to environmental politics.*

Liberal approaches to environmental politics is apparently well covered here. Conservative approaches are politically incorrect without a doubt, so why bother with them? Chairman Mao's Red Guards have disbanded. But Oberlin offers comparable training in independent analysis and intellectually balanced judgement.

America has many successful physicians, lawyers, engineers, pharmacists and teachers who happen to be African-American. But from the clamor at some of our universities about diversity, multiculturalism and affirmative action one could think that they are on the ramparts of a life-or-death struggle for equality. There are no places that are more race-conscious in America than some of its colleges and universities. Ultra-leftist faculty members try to stir up problems in order to offer "politically correct" – that is, Communist – solutions. This policy is no different than what the unlamented Soviet Union applied throughout the world during the Cold War.

African-Americans have made tremendous gains in higher education in the past decades. As *Washington Post* columnist William Raspberry pointed out recently, they will obtain an estimated 89,000 baccalaureate degrees in 1999, continuing a trend that saw an increase of 50 percent from 1976 to 1996. Today 11 percent of college students are African American, up from 8.8 percent in 1985. This needs some improvement, since among the college age generation of the U.S. 14.5 percent are African-American. Also, those already in college need to study toward professional and graduate degrees. Less than five percent of the nation's college faculty is African-American. There are great employment opportunities. But for an African-American student to wallow in the white ultra-liberal's race baiting and engage in pseudo-Marxist class warfare on campus is highly counterproductive.

WILLIAMS COLLEGE **English 355** <u>Theorizing Whiteness</u> - *This course examines "white" American identity as a cultural location. Among the questions we will ask: How does whiteness locate itself at the center of discourse, and how is it displaced? How does whiteness mask itself, and how does it disappear? What are the borders, visible and invisible, against which whiteness takes up its position? Do these borders ever shift? What does whiteness look like, sound like, and feel like from the perspective of the racial "other"? What happens when we consider whiteness as a racial or ethnic category? And in what ways do considerations of gender and class complicate these other questions? Authors to be considered include: Judith Butler, Roland Barthes, Chela Sandoval, Eric Lott, bell hooks, Cherrie Moraga, Ruth Frankenberg, James Baldwin, Homi Bhabha, Louisa May Alcott. Mark Twain, James Weldon Johnson, Charlotte Perkins Gilman, William Faulkner, Nathanael West, Alice Walker, and Don DeLillo.*

This analytic approach can be generalized: How does idiocy locate itself at the center of discourse, and how is it displaced? How does idiocy mask itself, and how does it disappear? What are the borders, visible and invisible, against which idiocy takes up its position? Do these borders ever shift? What does idiocy look like, sound like, and feel like from the perspective of the racial "other"? What happens when we consider idiocy as a racial or ethnic category?

MIDDLEBURY COLLEGE **American Literature 357** <u>Images of Blackness and Whiteness in American Literature</u>

VASSAR COLLEGE **Africana Studies 352b** <u>Seminar on Multiculturism in Comparative Perspective</u>

SWARTHMORE COLLEGE **Political Science 36** <u>Multicultural Politics in the U.S.: Democracy and Diversity</u>

SWARTHMORE COLLEGE **English Literature 85** <u>"Whiteness" and Racial Difference</u>

REED COLLEGE **Spanish 391** <u>Inscribing Identity in Chicano Literature</u>

AMHERST COLLEGE **Sociology 33** <u>Social Construction of the Self</u> - *This course brings together the perspectives of psychoanalysis, symbolic interactionism, developmental social psychology, as well as a variety of accounts in sociology, literature, and popular culture, to explore how a sense of self and identity develop in social life. Although the focus is on Western culture and traditions, we will be examining documentation provided by cross-cultural accounts in order to contextualize and problematize the truth claims of Western notions of identity construction and self-formation.*

In 1998 Amherst College charged $ 29,064 a year to teach a student sufficient dosage of "symbolic interactionism" to be able to "contextualize and problematize the truth claims of Western notions."

NEW YORK UNIVERSITY **Journalism and Mass Communi-cation V54.0016** <u>Minorities and the Media</u> - *Coverage of minorities and the relatively powerless continues to be one of the most sensitive areas in American journalism. Topics include the traditional basis of such coverage, how it changed during the civil rights upheaval of the 1960s and 1970s, what the prospects are for further change, and whether the mass media can ever truly serve and be responsive to the needs of a socially and economically diverse society. Examines in detail the effect that minority and women journalists have on their audiences and profession.*

COLUMBIA UNIVERSITY **History W3642x** <u>The Radical Tradition in America</u>

STANFORD UNIVERSITY **American Studies 164** <u>Introduction To Race And Ethnicity In The American Experience</u>

EMORY UNIVERSITY **Educational Studies 314** <u>Multicultural Education</u> - *The purpose of this seminar is to explore the meaning of culture, its influence on the "self" and "the other," as well as the influence of culture on issues of teaching and learning. This course centers around readings and a field component that explore sociopolitical factors as well as structural and cultural factors that influence the school achievement of students who come from diverse groups. This course is intended to give students a broad understanding of multicultural education through an exploration of issues related to culture, social class, ethnicity, andrace, gender, and language. Specific attention is given to an understanding of the history of - Asian Americans, Hispanics, African Americans, Native Americans, and Puerto Ricans.*

BROWN UNIVERSITY **Education 103** <u>The Psychology of Race, Class, and Gender</u> *This course focuses on the social construction of race, class, and gender and how this construction influences an individual's perception of self and other individuals. Some of the topics covered are identity development, achievement, motivation and sociopolitical development.*

DUKE UNIVERSITY **History 209S** Race, Class, and Gender in Modern British History. (CZ)

YALE UNIVERSITY **African and African-American Studies 112aG** New York Mambo: Microcosm of Black Creativity - *Rise, development, and philosophic achievement of the world of New York mambo and salsa. Emphasis on Palmieri, Cortijo, Roena, Harlow, and Colón. Examination of parallel traditions, e.g., New York Haitian art, Dominican merengue, reggae and rastas of Jamaican Brooklyn, and the New York school of Brazilian capoeira.*

UNIVERSITY OF PENNSYLVANIA **Afro-American Studies 603** American Racism   *The objective of this course is to enable students to identify racial contexts, historical and current, that frame the black American experience. Readings, class discussions, and assignments will encompass analysis of personal and professional experiences.*

UNIVERSITY OF PENNSYLVANIA **Afro-American Studies 642** Multiculturalism: Fieldwork/Theory

UNIVERSITY OF PENNSYLVANIA **Afro-American Studies 155** The Curse of Ham - *An examination of the development of biblical justification for the enslavement of Blacks and the historical context framing such development. The biblical "Curse of Ham," has been used for centuries to justify and explain the enslavement of Blacks in history. But, in fact, there is no such curse in the Bible. Why then, and how, did such a Curse develop? How was it imposed on, and integrated into, biblical tradition? Is it a Jewish creation? a Christian one? an Islamic one? What was the historical background on which the Curse developed? How, where, and when was it used historically? Providing context, the course examines views and attitudes toward black Africans as found in the ancient and medieval sources of the three Western religions: Judaism, Christianity and Islam. It also explores the relationship between these views and racism in Western civilization.*

Ambrose Bierce once wrote: "we wouldn't worry half so much what people thought about us, if we knew how seldom they did."

COLUMBIA UNIVERSITY **Music V3470** <u>Issues in Rock Music and Rock Culture</u> - *An ethnomusicological approach to issue in contemporary rock-and-roll culture, examining the significance of politics, gender, race, class, economics, censorship, stylistic development, the creative process, and group dynamics. Students will be required to conduct a small-scale fieldwork project in New York City.*

While talking about censorship, Columbia's administrators should explain why the November 14 - 15, 1998, conference entitled "Conservative Ideas in Higher Education" was literally chased off campus by self-righteous Leftist bully boys. These students of Columbia were taught to hold free speech and divergent ideas in contempt. It would be appropriate for the university bookstore to sell brown shirts.

PRINCETON UNIVERSITY **American Studies 327** <u>Race, Masculinity and the Rule of Law</u> - *An examination between the interplay of race and masculinity in American law. Topics include race; masculinity; national identity; legal ideology; contemporary far right political movements; the construction of criminality; and Multiculturalism. Materials include court decisions, transcripts of trials, scholarly articles, novels, and films.*

SYRACUSE UNIVERSITY **History 346** <u>The Idea of Opportunity in America, 1890-1940</u> - *Diverse contemporary perspectives on American opportunity—and its limits—from the closing of the frontier through the Great Depression. Tensions and possibilities resulting from urbanization, immigration, technological advances, persistent conservatism, reform, and radical impulses.*

SYRACUSE UNIVERSITY **Philosophy 379** <u>American Slavery and the Holocaust</u> - *An in-depth study of the normative structure* *of both American Slavery and the Holocaust, focusing upon the ways in which each institution conceived of its victims and the character of the moral climate that prevailed in each case.*

Senior editor of *Commentary* magazine, Gabriel Schoenfeld remarked in *The New York Times*:

"today, with the emergence of a new discipline called 'Holocaust studies,' the academization of the subject is proceeding apace, complete with meaningless jargon and political agenda-setting. Where one leading scholar pronounces the Holocaust 'a multidimensional, many-person event,' another contends that it offers grounds for 'non-objectivist, anti-positivist, feminist objectivity.' The titles of papers delivered at the 29th Annual Holocaust Scholars' Conference...[March, 1999]—'An Afrocentric Critique of the Diary of Anne Frank,' 'Pop Art Representations of the Holocaust,' the 'Holocaust and Femicide/Female Feticide'—give an all too keen sense of the academic fashions that have taken hold of the field."

The "feminazis," to use Rush Limbaugh's term, are on the march in academia. Although many of their claims about being victimized by men are false, they carry on with their man-hating propaganda. For instance, the ultra-liberal American Association of University Women's often mentioned 1992 report about girls being shortchanged in schools was proven utterly false. In fact, girls are doing better than boys, and their numbers in colleges are growing at a rate that alarms educators. In 1996 55 percent of undergraduates in America were young women. The U. S. Department of Education projects that in 2007 only 6.9 million men will be in college, compared to 9.1 million women, almost 57 percent. In 1870, over a hundred years ago, 85.3 percent of bachelor degrees were awarded to men. In 1996 this number dropped to 44.9 percent. The 2007 projection is 42.0 percent. Obviously, men are turned off by the anti-men, politicized campus atmosphere and the drastic reduction of market-value of college degrees. It this trend doesn't change we will need affirmative action programs favoring white males at the nations' universities. They can then demand their segregated dormitories and courses in White Studies. Full circle.

A roster of high schools' top performers, *Who's Who Among American High-school Students,* consistently recognizes more girls than boys. According to a recent *Wall Street Journal* article by education professor Diane Ravitch of New York University, boys are 50 percent more likely to repeat a grade than girls. And about the feminist complaints concerning girls' *self esteem:* boys are five times more likely to commit suicide than girls. More than two thirds of special education students are boys. More boys are stuffed full of Ritalin™ than girls. Perhaps we have way too many female teachers in our primary and secondary schools who favor their own gender. Handing teaching certificates to retiring chief petty officers of our nuclear Navy and letting them teach in our elementary and high schools would drastically improve the situation.

In America, women contribute 38 percent to Social Security and collect 52 percent of the benefits. In 1993 Congress appropriated $ 400 million for research on breast cancer which kills 42,000 women annually, but only $ 39 million for research on prostate cancer, which kills 40,000 men annually. These are hardly indications of discrimination against women.

In spite of all such examples, courses on feminism and gender politics are high on the agenda at several elite schools. Here is a sample of their offerings:

STANFORD UNIVERSITY **Anthropology 147A** <u>Comparative Feminism</u> - *Interdisciplinary seminar for upper-level undergrad-*

uates. Women's struggles for empowerment, situating them in the specific cultural and historical contexts in which they have emerged in different parts of the world. Focus: broaden an understanding of women's struggles in the world, and develop analytical models that enable study of these struggles in their complexities and specificities by calling into question dominant assumptions about feminism.

UNIVERSITY OF CHICAGO **Gender Studies 289/389** <u>Fetishism, Gender, Sexuality, and Capitalism</u> -*This course analyzes transformations in the cultural construction of gendered and sexed identities in Japan, Europe, and the United States in nineteenth and twentieth centuries. Starting with readings from Marx and Freud on the commodity form and fetish, we read critiques and re-uses of these concepts from feminist and queer theory. We then analyze a series of case studies from our three geographic areas. Possible cases include advertising and display strategies; kleptomania as a diagnosis and theft as a political gesture; style and political mobilization in feminist and gay/lesbian/queer politics. Questions of the relation of structure and agency and the possibilities for emancipatory politics are considered throughout.*

REED COLLEGE **Classics 314** <u>Gender and Sexuality in the Classical World</u> - *Full course for one semester. Introduction to feminist theory and its application to classical culture. We will examine how male and female are constructed, how literature and literary criticism participate in this process, the possibility of resistance to gender codes, and the role of cosmetics and cross-dressing. The main focus will be late Republican and Imperial Rome, but some criticism will focus on earlier periods. Classical readings will include such works as Sulpicia's elegies, Ovid's Heroides, Cicero's letters, and Plautus' comedies; critical works will be drawn from both inside and outside classical studies, including the work of Judith Butler, Eve Sedgwick, Michel Foucault, and Amy Richlin.*

CORNELL UNIVERSITY **English 427** <u>Studies in Shakespeare: Gender, Sexuality, Cultural Politics</u> - *The seminar will focus on*

Shakespeare's drama and poetry to examine questions of gender and sexuality in their historical context. Texts will include The Rape of Lucrece, Twelfth Night, The Merchant of Venice, Measure for Measure, The Taming of the Shrew, Hamlet, Othello, Antony and Cleopatra, Coriolanus, The Sonnets. Discussions will address many issues: cross-dressing, masculine identity, the situation of women, royal politics, market economies, sumptuary law, anti-theatrical pamphlets. Students will also be introduced to representative critical approaches and debates in Shakespeare studies (feminist, new historical, queer, post-structuralist, psychoanalytic) and will write a critical research paper.

DARTMOUTH COLLEGE **Women's Studies 45** <u>Adored, Admired, and Despised: Women in Pop Music and Music Video</u> - *Music video and pop music disseminate images of women to a vast media audience. These images are myth, representation, and self-representation, arch-type, and stereotype. How do we read and categorize them? Is there an emergent pattern within genres? What role do the producers and consumers of these images play? The aim of this course is to question the images of women in music video by means of a theoretical framework of essays and articles taken from visual theory. We will work toward an understanding of how and why the representation of women in music video operates on its audience.*

DARTMOUTH COLLEGE **Women's Studies 43** <u>Shakespeare and Gender</u>

WELLESLEY COLLEGE **Political Science 344** <u>Feminist Political Theory</u> - *Examination of 19th and 20th century feminist theory with focus on contemporary debates. The feminist critique of liberalism and socialism will introduce discussion of issues such as methodology, gender differences, race, and sexuality. Authors read will include Mill, Marx, Engels, and the contemporary theorists Alison Jagger, Sandra Harding, Carol Gilligan, and Catherine MacKinnon.*

NEW YORK UNIVERSITY **Africana Studies V11.0315 Twentieth Century Black Feminist Thought and Practice in the U.S.**

DARTMOUTH COLLEGE **College Courses 22** <u>The Masculine Mystique</u> - *Why are so many boys and men fascinated by sports and war? Why are Sylvester Stallone and Arnold Schwarzenegger cult movie heroes? Why are young boys more threatened by the term "sissy" than girls are by the term "tomboy"? What are the distinctive qualities of men's friendships with other men and of their intimate relationships with women? Why do so many men describe their relationships with their fathers as troubled? Are our conceptions of masculinity dominated by models of white male development? What is the connection of biological sex with contemporary western notions of masculinity? Using gender studies as an enabling methodology and drawing on two academic disciplines - education and literary analysis, or, more specifically, adolescent psychology and literary criticism - this course will explore these and other questions. We will draw on contemporary research in the psychology of boy's and girl's development, case studies written by college students, and major literary texts. Readings from anthropology, sociolinguistics, sociology, and race and ethnic studies, and movies will be utilized in this interdisciplinary and multicultural course.*

COLUMBIA UNIVERSITY **Anthropology V3951** <u>Pirates, Boys, and Capitalism</u> - *Through a detailed analysis of the history and figure of the pirate in the Western imagination, the course asks why the pirate exerts such appeal through the ages and therewith aims at introducing students to the key problems in anthropological and culture theory concerning colonialism, violence.*

How did those bad, bad boys get into these things? ... Again.

HARVARD UNIVERSITY **Sociology 207** <u>Gender and Sexuality</u> - *Argues that "gender" and "sexuality" are neither fixed in real-*

ity nor free floating in space but rather institutionalized in a limited set of dynamic cultural and organizational arrangements, such as the state and science. The configuration of these arrangements sets the boundaries within which gender and sexuality have meaning and motivate action in society at large.

Would someone really want to have a bachelor degree in gobbledegook from Harvard?

CARNEGIE MELLON UNIVERSITY **Philosophy 80-341** <u>Race, Gender, and Justice</u> - *The first part of this course examines social ideas of equality and justice and challenges them with the current realities of racial, gender, and cultural conflict (e.g., discrimination and sexual harassment). Communication styles and attitudes, opposing values and agendas, and unmet expectations produce and escalate many damaging and intransigent conflicts in the U.S. In the second part of the course, we explore possible strategies for addressing the conflicts and moving forward collaboratively. How are businesses, schools, and communities responding to diversity and culturalism, and are the responses effective? We will look at several widely used approaches, including legal suits, affirmative action, conflict resolution, diversity training, and multicultural education, to see whether they meet the needs of the affected people and to ask whether they entail changes in our understanding of fundamental values such as justice.*

"Three strikes and you are out," and "10, 20, life" should have been added to this list. One must try to remember that Carnegie-Mellon is one of the foremost universities in the field of computer science. Luckily, when one studies professional subjects, there is no room on one's schedule to take junk like these courses.

AMHERST COLLEGE **Women's and Gender Studies 14** <u>Ingrate Books: Chartering and Un-chartering Patriarchy</u> - *The European canon tells and retells the heroic tale of how males took charge of heaven and earth. We shall consider the formation of* *that ancient tradition from the perspective of modern works that revise, debunk, or reverse the parable. Classic texts will be paired with modern retellings or equivalents: Homer's Odyssey with Christine Bell, The Perez Family; The Homeric Hymns to Demeter with Jenny Joseph, Persephone; Aeschylus Oresteia with Emily Bronte, Wuthering Heights; Plato's Symposium with Henry James, The Bostonians; Virgil's Aeneid with Willa Cather, A Lost Lady and The Professor's House.*

We shall examine how the subordination of female to male supports other ranked categories: mind/body, rational/irrational, public/private, heaven/earth, order/disorder. How do these hierarchies justify violence (rape, intra-familial murder, human sacrifice, silencing) in founding and maintaining the cultural order? How does the emergence of (homo) sexualities, ancient and modern, undermine the authority of this collective society; laughter as a form of revolt; the "thaw" after Stalin's death; and the demise of the Soviet Union in 1991. Readings include the short novels - A. Kollontai's Love of Worker Bee, E. Zamyatin's We, and A. Solzhenitsyn's One Day in the Life of Ivan Denisovich, V. Mayakovsky's play Bed Bug, and essays on film and culture. Weekly viewings of slides and Russian films. No knowledge of Russian required.

SYRACUSE UNIVERSITY **Philosophy 297** <u>Philosophy of Feminism</u>

WILLIAMS COLLEGE **Economics 355** <u>Feminist Economics</u> - *Neoclassical economics appears not to have much to say about gender: its tools purport to be gender-neutral and its framework universal. But a growing movement of feminist economists argue that this universality is illusory; neoclassical economics is based on a number of highly gendered assumptions that we often take for granted. These assumptions affect how we choose what is considered valuable economic activity, how we expect people to make decisions, and how we expect people to behave in different situations (for example, in the market vs. at home). Recently, there has been a profusion of research, both theoretical and empirical, challenging these assumptions. We will examine research* *by feminist economists on a variety of topics, including (but not limited to) household decision-making, women in development, balancing paid and unpaid labor, gendered images in economics texts and articles, and welfare reform.*

WILLIAMS COLLEGE **Political Science 306S** Practicing Feminism: A Study of Political Activism - *This course will explore the issues and problems of putting feminism into practice. What constraints and opportunities confront feminists as they struggle for social change? What are the sources of and limits on their power? How and when do they choose to compromise and negotiate or object and fight? How are these issues represented in the culture through the press, through other media, through art? We will examine issues such as organizational dynamics, budgetary and administrative constraints, client-staff interactions, power and dependency, and mother-child-family relationships. Students will do fieldwork at community agencies involved in health care, social services, and work. A variety of interactions with these organizations are encouraged, ranging from administrative and service work to public art projects that might raise awareness of feminist issues in the community.*

In the 1960s Williams College, a former single sex school, was celebrated for its social maturity when it banned fraternities prior to its turn into a coeducational institution. It came a long way. If a female student was one out of four applicants lucky enough to get accepted, she can now go about raising awareness of feminist issues in her home town. For this potential social embarrassment, the charge for tuition, room and board for a year was $ 29,360 in 1998.

SWARTHMORE COLLEGE **Political Science 13** Feminist Political Theory - *Contemporary feminism transforms central questions of political theory. Some of the most creative theorizing is taking place in feminist legal theory. This course explores key contributions and debates in feminist political and legal theory. While focusing chiefly upon western theory, the course engages feminists from non-western cultures on the capacity of western* *feminists to speak to different experiences. The course considers feminist examinations of human nature; the body in political theory; personhood and citizenship; voice and the law; theorizing otherness; discourses privileged and silenced; limits of privacy: relationships between power, sexuality, race and identity.*

Homosexuality occurs in about five percent of the American people. Today it is an accepted condition, no less than astigmatism. Medicine, as of now, cannot cure it, mainline churches do not condemn it. Most people, however, are not ready to celebrate it, as some colleges are bent on doing. Sexually deviant behaviors fascinate some faculty members at our best colleges. Some may even get caught at them. This writer was about to make a crack recommending that pederasty be included in the curricula of our elite institutions, when Accuracy in Academia's *Campus Report* published the followings:

CORNELL UNIVERSITY offers <u>The Sexual Child</u>, a class requiring pro-pedophilia readings and the viewing of pictures of naked children. A typical assignment complains, *"boy lovers are so stigmatized that it is difficult to find defenders for their civil liberties, let alone erotic orientation."* Opposing *"cross generational encounters,"* students learn, has *"more in common with ideologies of racism than with true ethics."* The poor dears, what can they do now? Perhaps they should complain to the federal government about discrimination.

Well, OK, they already have courses about pedophilia. But how about a few offerings on the "Theory and Practice of Necrophilia?" Certainly, the American taxpayer will be delighted to finance it.

Here are some of the most deviant examples of course offerings:

SWARTHMORE COLLEGE **English Literature 90** Queer Media - *How are sexual identities 'mediated' by popular culture? How do lesbian and gay film and video makers 'queer' sexual norms and standard media forms? Drawing on gay and lesbian cultural theorists Roland Barthes, Judith Butler, Teresa de Lauretis, Richard Dyer, Michel Foucault, Isaac Julien, and Pier Paolo Pasolini, we will challenge classic Hollywood's heterosexual presumption and the recent mass media exploitation of lesbian and gay culture and theorize lesbian and a aesthetic strategies and modes of address in a number of contexts: the American avant-garde (Kenneth Anger, Andy Warhol, Su Friedrich); international auteurs (R.W. Fassbinder, Chantal Akerman); gay liberation and AIDS activism (Word is Out, Zero Patience); women's cinema (Lizzie Borden, Michelle Parkerson, Lordes Portillo), multicultural and diasporan film and video (Shu Lea Cheang, Richard Fung, Isaac Julien) and the new queer cinema (Tom Kahn, Rose Troche).*

COLUMBIA UNIVERSITY **History W3685y** Introduction to the history of homosexuality in the West

YALE UNIVERSITY **Women's and Gender Studies 485a** Feminist and Queer Theory - *Examination of current theoretical work on gender and sexuality, in their interaction with other systems of identity and differentiation. Emphasis on comparative perspectives and on the consequences of theory.*

The American military's ROTC program was labeled unfit to meet in Yale's lecture halls. Good thing too. Yale graduates might corrupt America's defense establishment after they are exposed to this type of education. "Don't ask, don't tell." but sodomists are still not welcome.

HARVARD UNIVERSITY **English 197** Lesbian and Gay Studies

AMHERST COLLEGE **English 91** Black Gay Fiction - *This course will examine fictional and non-fictional texts of gay and* *lesbian black writers in the United States. We will pay close attention to identity politics and how they are articulated in these texts. In addition to examining these works, we will also read a number of theorists who offer "queer" readings of "canonical" texts. The course readings might include works by Essex Hemphill, Becky Birtha, April Sinclair, Audre Lorde, E. Lynn Harris, bell hooks, Larry Duplechan, Derek Scott, Bessie Smith, Marlon Riggs, Barbara Smith, James Baldwin, Cheryl Clark, Isaac Julien, and Kobena Mercer.*

DARTMOUTH COLLEGE **Drama 20** <u>Gay and Lesbian Theater since Stonewall</u> - *This course will explore gay and lesbian drama and performance since that epochal moment in queer history, the Stonewall riots. Taking Mart Crowley's "The Boys in the Band" as our starting point, we will examine how and why queer theatre in America and Britain developed an '"out" aesthetic. What dramaturgical strategies did this kind of theater use to subvert the sexual status quo? Is queer theatre inherently political? What social and cultural purpose did it serve for its gay and lesbian audiences? Some of the playwrights, theatre troupes, and theatre spaces we will examine include Joe Orton, Mare Irene Fornes, Harvey Fierstein, WOW Café, Charles Ludlum, and the Ridiculous Theater, Holly Hughes, Tony Kushner, Paula Vogel, Porno Afro Homos, Larry Kramer, Split Britches, Bloolips, and Tim Miller. Theoretical readings will include essays by Jill dolan, Alisa Solomon, D.A. Miller, Susan Sontag, and Judith Butler.*

VASSAR COLLEGE **English 388** <u>Gay Male Fiction in America Since 1945</u> - *Can one speak meaningfully of "gay male fiction" as a genre? If so, what exactly constitutes the genre? What are its antecedents, its roots, its influences? Who are its practitioners, its audience, its politics? Writers will include Gore Vidal, James Baldwin, Edmund White, Andrew Holleran, Christopher Bram, Dennis Cooper, William Burroughs, Mark Merlis, and Scott Heim. Writing assignments are both creative and analytical.*

CORNELL UNIVERSITY **English 377** <u>Gay Fiction</u> - *This course offers an overview of male homoerotic narratives in literature and film. We will examine a number of texts from different* *historical and cultural sources to discuss the literary and cinematic construction of desire between men. The course is organized around the various personae who have been the most influential historical paradigms for the articulation of modern gay identity. Topics for discussion will include Platonic and Christian idealism, sublimation, sexual encoding, the gay outlaw, decadence, psychoanalyses, AIDS and desire, and identification across race, class, generation, and sexual orientation. We will discuss texts by Plato, Christopher Marlowe, Sigmund Freud, Thomas Mann, Tennessee Williams, Jean Genet, Manuel Puig, Alan Hollinghurst, Caryl Churchill, and Tony Kushner, as well as films by Pier Paolo Pasolini, Derek Jarman, Pedro Almodovar, Rosa von Praunheim, Todd Haynes, and Marlon Riggs, among others. Attendance at weekly film screenings is required.*

SWARTHMORE COLLEGE English Literature 71K <u>Lesbian Novels Since World War Two</u>

BROWN UNIVERSITY Afro-American Studies 99 <u>Black Lavender: Study of Black Gay/Lesbian Plays</u> - *An interdisciplinary approach to the study of plays that address the identities and issues of Black gay men and lesbians, and offer various points of view from within and without the Black gay and lesbian artistic communities. The focus is on primary analysis of unpublished titles~ also included for research are published titles by Amiri Baraka, Ed Bullins, P.J. Gibson, Cheryl West, Shay Youngblood, and Porno Afro Homos. In-person, phone, and email interviews with playwrights, directors, actors, and producers.*

COLUMBIA UNIVERSITY Sociology V3310x <u>Gender and Deviance</u>

YALE UNIVERSITY Women's and Gender Studies 296b <u>Introduction to Lesbian and Gay Studies</u> - *A study of works that have as their main theme gay and lesbian experience and identity in the twentieth-century United States. They include fiction and autobiographical texts, historical and sociological materials, queer theory, and films, focusing on modes of representing sexu-*

ality and on the intersections between sexuality and race, ethnicity, class, gender, and nationality.

BUCKNELL UNIVERSITY **English 228** <u>Gay/Lesbian/Bisexual Studies</u>

CORNELL UNIVERSITY **English 279** <u>Lesbian Personae</u> - *This course will offer a survey of literature and films by and about lesbians. We will examine how lesbian desire and identity are historically constructed through narrative. What does it mean to read as a lesbian? What are the various tropes and personae through which lesbian desire has been articulated? What has been the relationship of lesbianism to feminism? How is lesbian identity inflected by homophobia, sexism, racism? We will begin with a look at early paradigms for lesbian desire such as romantic friendship and sexual inversion, then move on to an extensive examination of lesbian feminism, and close with a discussion of desire and performativity. We will read fiction by Gertrude Stein, Radclyffe Hall, Havelock Ellis, Sigmund Freud, Nella Larsen, Adrienne Rich, Monique Wittig, Alice Walker, Cherrie Moraga, Jeanette Winterson, and Djuna Barnes, as well as films by Leontine Sagan, Monica Truet, and Rainer Werner Fassbinder among others. Students will be expected to attend a weekly film screening in addition to seminars.*

BROWN UNIVERSITY **English 115** <u>Studies in Sexuality</u>

WILLIAMS COLLEGE **English 341** <u>American Genders, American Sexualities</u>

Williams boasts a truly enviable student/faculty ratio: 8. With so many faculty members at hand, running out of topics worthy to teach must be a nagging problem. With the increase in globalization one wonders when courses on Canadian genders and German sexualities will find their way through the faculty committees.

UNIVERSITY OF CHICAGO **History 287/387** <u>Nation: Feminist/queer Politics and Theory</u>

Benefactor John D. Rockefeller must be gyrating in his grave.

DUKE UNIVERSITY **English JOJD** <u>Perspectives in Gay, Lesbian, and Bisexual Studies</u>

WELLESLEY COLLEGE **Women's Studies 317** <u>History of Sexuality: Queer Theory</u> - *Will introduce the concepts central to queer theory, starting with Foucault and Laqueur and discussions of sexual difference and deviance. It will examine queerness in its various manifestations and practices, butch-femme, transgendering, cross-dressing, bisexuality, and third gender. The conflicts and continuities between identity politics and queer identities will be explored in the context of racialization, class, and different abledness and under the markers if nationhood and subalternity. Finally, what impact do the debates on the production of sexuality in different sites and historical periods have on theories of queerness.*

OBERLIN COLLEGE **Theater and Dance 270** <u>Special Topics in Gender and Performance: Queer Acts</u>

VASSAR COLLEGE **Philosophy 280b** <u>Queer Theory: Choreographics of Sex and Gender</u>

STANFORD UNIVERSITY **Feminist Studies 240** <u>Lesbian Communities and Identities</u> - *Scholarship and research on lesbian experience. Issues of homophobia, lesbian intimacy and sexuality, femme and butch roles, lesbian separatism, and diversity of lesbian communities and identities.*

Teaching trash disguised as art is not limited to leading Ivy schools. The *St. Petersburg Times*[3] reported that a UNIVERSITY OF SOUTH FLORIDA teaching assistant was temporarily reassigned following a sexual harassment complaint by a female student in an 'Introduction to Art' course designed for non-art majors. The student objected to a picture shown by the instructor to the class in which he was engaged in a sexual act. It was ostensibly an example of potentially controversial art. The picture's title was "N... screwing white woman." Within a week the student withdrew from the course, upon which the instructor was reinstated to the applause of his students. Case closed.

The last gem in this lamentable roster is from an article by writer Kim Ash.[4] She described the experience of an "A" student of music at EASTERN ILLINOIS UNIVERSITY (no ivy there) after taking **Music 3562C** which is supposed to expose students to Asian, African and South American folk art and music. The student decided to sue the university in order to get her tuition back after she was confronted with numerous examples of "controversial artistic expression." It included a photo of two men drinking enemas from each other's bodies and a photocopied image depicting a man who has supposedly amputated his penis. As the student had to complete the course before she could start her practice teaching, she was not amused.

The 25 campuses whose course descriptions were reviewed for this chapter are rightfully considered the jewels of America's higher education. Most of the professors teaching at these schools are well-qualified academics who maintain high scholastic standards. In spite of the presence

3   November 5, 1999

4   *Washington Times, National Weekly Edition,*
     February 1 - 7, 1999.

of a small but noisy group of weirdos, there is still a great body of knowledge available at these schools. But one has to be cautious. It is like visiting Key West. People go there to enjoy the sunset, key lime pie, conch chowder and the general ambience of the raw bars. Getting infected with AIDS is optional.

These highly-esteemed universities and colleges are over-subscribed each year by a factor of five to ten. One wonders how for the number of applications would fall if parents and prospective students were aware of what is being taught at these schools, how the Ivy League and its imitators are poisoning young minds. All it would take, really, is a look into the college catalogs.

It is not to say that such smut courses are limited to these ivy covered halls. In addition to the two examples, such courses are all over. One finds them even at some of the nation's supposedly conservative Catholic colleges. Looking at these course descriptions individually gives the impression that they spend a bit too much attention to insignificant, minor issues. But the composite picture portrays a full scale attack against values traditionally held in common among Americans. Syndicated columnist Charley Reese hit it on the head when he wrote:

"An educational system designed to graduate semiliterate, young socialists who are atheistic and hostile to their own country, to capitalism and to liberty is not a system sensible Americans would want their children involved in."

Reese may have thought of the elite schools quoted on these pages. How frightening the situation is was spelled out by best-selling British novelist William Diehl in the following words:

"What's happening is that we are living in a world full of people who want us to think the way they do and act the way they do and believe the way they do and if we don't, if we don't conform, they destroy us. And you know the irony? They're always in the minority. We ignore them until we wake up one morning and there isn't any *Times* on the newsstand and our favorite books are gone from the library and they beat up our best friends and drag them off to prison because their hair's the wrong color or their noses don't measure down to their standards. Then it's too late."

10. The Ed-Biz

No matter what colleges and universities would do to correct their programs, their work will be greatly hindered unless major improvements are made in the quality of their incoming freshmen. The general college requirements, some places called "core programs," should, to a large extent, be pushed down into the graduating requirements of high schools. This would not only shorten the academic programs at the college level, but also reduce, if not eliminate the excessive amount of remedial work currently carried out at the great majority of universities. A drastic improvement of high school preparation would particularly help professional programs that are already operating well in excess of the common college graduation requirement of 120 semester credits. But unless universities, and parents, force the K - 12 establishment to do something about this, improvements are unlikely to be made.

One would assume that a nation's high schools' minimum graduation requirement would be a basic knowledge of her history. This is not so in America. In December, 1999, the American Council of Trustees and Alumni sponsored a survey[1] conducted by the University of Connecticut at 55 of the nation's top colleges including Harvard and Princeton, on 556 randomly selected seniors. Nearly 80 percent of the respondents received failing grades, D or F, on 35 questions on American history. A measly 22 percent knew that the Gettysburg Address contained the phrase " government of the people, by the people, for the people." Only 35 percent

1   Associated Press, June 28, 2000.

of the students knew that the Korean war started under the presidency of Truman. One-third didn't know that it was Patrick Henry who wrote "give me liberty of give me death." More than a third did not know the Constitution established the division of power in U.S. Government, and only 23 percent identified James Madison as the principal framer of the Constitution. The report found that none of the 55 colleges required a course on American history for graduation. Senator Joseph Lieberman lamented the findings. Quoting Jefferson, he said that "if a nation expects to be ignorant and free it expects what never was and never will be." Of course, legislating American history graduating requirement at the nation's colleges would be a stupid idea. Legislating mandatory graduation requirements, including American history, at high schools would be the way to go.

In his autobiography[2], a retired vice president of Lear Jet describes his trip on the Railroad with his grown daughter:

> "Our trip was during the days of Gorbachev with communism still in full bloom. Lenin statues and pictures were in abundance no matter where you looked. At every small station there was at least one statue of Lenin. After a few days of this, my daughter, a typical product of the American educational system, which means they learn nothing about nothing, asked one of the Soviet girl-guides accompanying our group: "Who the hell is this guy Lenin anyway?" (Like asking the Pope, who in hell is Jesus Christ?) The Russian girl was duly shocked, after all Lenin was their God. I wonder what she thought of her barbarian tourists."

2   Sandor (Alex) Kvassay: *Alex in Wonderland,*
     Tucson: Westernlore, 1995.

Complaints about education in the United States have a long history. Richard Mitchell wrote in 1981:

> "The problems and disorders in education have became more and more visible in the last few years, of course, and even the ordinary citizen who happens to have no children in the schools suspects that something is very wrong , but he will never understand exactly *what* is wrong until he realizes that all our educational problems and disorders, none of which are new, although they *are* more obvious, provide endless and growing employment for the people who made them. Barely literate children may be suffering and facing whole lives of deprivation, but consultants and remediationists and professors of reading education and tax supported researchers and the editors and publishers of workbooks and handsome packets of materials are doing very well indeed and looking for even better days to come. It is important to note, too, that all these profit-makers have not suddenly appeared among us like the wandering bands of looters who can reasonably be expected to show up after the earthquake. They have been around a long time, diligently turning the wheel, professing what must be remediated and remediating what has been professed and enlarging in our society the role of what can only be called the educationist-industrial complex. Anything that may seem to us a disorder in education is for them a golden opportunity – indeed, since they live by tax money, they cannot make their profits until we *do* see a disorder in education and feel obliged to shell out.

> "Curiously enough, therefore, it is very much in the interest of the policymakers and theoreticians of public schooling that there *be* problems and failures and that we know about them and also, even more curiously, that *any* kind of social disorder at all be made the business of the schools." [3]

In the opinion of the chancellor of New York City's schools, Harold O. Levy:

"The quality of teachers has been declining for decades, and no one wants to talk about it. Principals know the truth and have to deal with it as best as they can, but unions are reluctant to admit weaknesses in any of their members, colleges are loath to acknowledge the poor quality of their education programs, and administrators are afraid that confronting the problem will further erode confidence in public education. ... Which of our college-age students, today, are preparing for teaching? A 1997 report by the National Center for Education Statistics found that education majors were placed in remedial college courses at higher rates than their counterparts in the humanities and social sciences – nearly twice as many education majors needed remedial English and math classes." [4]

Math and science are the most critical subjects for the nation. These are the areas where teacher incompetence does the most damage. Sadly, it is easy to became a certified teacher with no basic concept of what mathematics is all about. Many students of teachers' colleges were first flunked out of other fields, quite often for lack of mathematics skills. In many school districts in America, a teacher can teach through eighth grade with an elementary teacher certificate that does not require specialization. How could one expect students in American public schools to be able to even understand basic mathematical concepts like algebra and geometry in ninth grade if they were taught by a bunch of math incompetents?

3   Ritchard Mitchell: *The Graves of Academe;*
     Little, Brown, 1981

4   Harold O. Levy: *Strive for excellence in
     teaching, New York Times,* September 10, 2000

Allowing people who know math and science to enter teaching as a second career has long been resisted by the educrats. There are fewer than ten universities in the country offering accelerated programs retraining people who know mathematics and science but do not have a background in education. The concept is a threat to the education colleges.

Colleges throughout the land are forced to teach algebra and geometry to their students because they failed to learn it in junior high school. In the state of Florida, for instance, more than four out of ten high school graduates who entered a state college in 1998 needed remedial classes because they were not ready for college. The cost to the state? Roughly $ 12 million. In the California State University system, fully 54 percent of entering freshmen were forced to take remedial math in the fall of 1998, 47 percent needed remedial English. Altogether, 70 percent of the freshmen needed some type of class to bring their skills up to college level proficiency, costing the state of California $ 10 million yearly.

Teacher incompetence was qualitatively demonstrated in the spring of 1998 in Massachusetts when, for the first time, applicants for new teaching jobs had to take a test for basic competence in reading, writing and a subject area. Fifty-nine percent of the applicants failed. Of the 56 institutions where the test-takers came from, students of some very highly regarded institutions such as Brandeis (57 percent) had spectacular failure rates. The University of Massachusetts at Amherst — where all those insipid multicultural education courses mentioned earlier are offered — had a 45 percent failure rate. Projecting this to the 3.1 million teachers in America leads to the dismal conclusion that many of them do not belong in the classroom. However, the profession is strictly controlled by highly politicized unions mandating across-the-board raises, uniform salary scales, and tenure that protects the incompetents. Rather than facing the need to dismantle the existing system of financing, staffing and managing our high schools and putting it into order, American education accedes to its disastrous condition and blithely passes the problem on to the colleges whose admissions standards are lowered to meet the "need."

The situation is getting worse. Americans who graduated some 40 years ago were first among the 29 industrialized nations of the world with a graduation rate of 77 percent — from a curriculum much tougher than it is today. In 1998 America had the second-to-worst graduation rate among the 29, just above Mexico. Based on gross national product (GNP), our expenditure for teachers is the lowest. It shows.

Incompetent teachers can't keep order in grade school classrooms. In their utter boredom, young boys brimming with energy, act up. The schools solve the problem by drugging them with Ritalin, whose production increased seven-fold since 1990. Political dissidents in the Soviet Union were sent to mental institutions and got similar treatment.

The problem of shortage of competent mathematics teachers spills over to the fields of science. According to a 1998 report by the U. S. Department of Education, only 20 percent of 4,049 teachers surveyed nationally felt competent to teach science or technology. This conveys that the great majority of teachers are, intellectually, in the pre-industrial age. This explains another problem in our schools: while classrooms are increasingly equipped with computers, many teachers are ill equipped to use them as instructional tools. A recent U.S. Department of Education survey indicated that only 20 percent of classroom teachers felt they can use computer technology in their teaching. But while schools spend, on the average, about $ 88 per student on computers, only $ 6 per student is spent on training the teachers how to use them. While the country's 87,000 schools had about 6 million computers and about 80 percent had Internet access by the end of 1998 most teachers were not ready to make use of them. The situation is most critical in schools of low income areas.

Glenn T. Seaborg, two other Nobel Laureates, and 30 other scientists offered to write a K - 12 science curriculum for the state of California, gratis. They were turned down, and the contract given to a group of professional educators for $178,000 reports Martin Gross[5]:

"The educators charged that Seaborg et al. were pushing traditional science, which they feared was "too elitist." Their proof? "Science was dominated by white males."

Low-income minority students have particular difficulty with mathematics. According to University of Texas professor Philip Uri Treisman, an expert in teaching freshman calculus to low income minorities, "there was no year in a decade at Berkeley in which two black kids got a B or better in calculus." There is a particular poignancy to this, as the University of California at Berkeley is one of the leading "activist" schools of the nation. One would think they would do something about this problem.

<hr>

5   Martin L. Gross: *The Conspiracy of Ignorance,*
New York: Harper Collins, 1999.

It is not surprising that deficiency in mathematics skills is also endemic in the American work force. According to a 1998 survey of 1,054 companies by the American Management Association, 58,867 out of 165,684 job applicants were deficient in mathematics and reading skills. That is one in three applicants. Among the 20,000 employees of Owens Corning Company in Toledo, Ohio, 20 to 30 percent were found to perform at third or fourth grade level in basic math and reading skills. To be able to operate a proposed company-wide computer system, at least eighth-grade level performance would be necessary.

There is a great deal of talk about the coming technological age. Mostly columnists and TV commentators talk about it. Presidential candidates promise greater access to colleges and give lip service to needed educational improvements. The simple fact is that over 43 percent of the nation is composed of people who were not even capable of, or interested in finishing high school. That is the real problem in American education.

With America's current educational establishment — the faculties of the schools of education perpetrating ignorance, the state and federal bureaucrats keeping a strangle-hold, and the teachers' unions sabotaging proposed improvements — not much will happen. The failure of can public schools has already been well documented.[6] There has been a great deal of finger-pointing in trying to find the reasons for the failings of America's high schools. There is plenty of blame to go around. Those who really deserve the

6   Martin L. Gross:: *Conspiracy of Ignorance*, New
     York: Harper Collins, 1999.

blame are American taxpayers who are willing to put up with the situation. It is now time for the President and the U.S. Congress to take the curriculum out of local control, claiming national emergency. It would be a rightful claim.

Unfortunately, in each presidential election recently Americans vote for a self-styled "education president." In 1993, for instance, the Clinton administration's *Goals 2000* asserted that by 2000, America's high school graduation rate will be 90 percent and American students would lead the world in mathematics and science achievements. Nothing has happened. So much for politicians' promises.

In 1910 one of America's most innovative educators, Abraham Flexner, submitted a very critical report to the Carnegie Foundation on the quality of 155 medical schools in the United States and Canada. It had an immediate and sensational impact on American medical education. Many of the colleges severely criticized by Flexner closed soon after the release of the report. Others initiated extensive revisions of their curricula and educational policies. That was the beginning of modern medical education in America. In the 1920s, working for the Rockefeller Foundation, he collected several billions dollars in today's money from private donors for the improvement of American medical education. Where is a Flexner, or a Rockefeller, when we need one?

Columnist Charley Reese[7] put it well:

7   Public education beyond reform, King Features
     Syndicate, Sep. 20, 2000.

"... children finish secondary school for the most part totally unprepared to make a living. Most are unprepared for higher education. This is despite the fact that universities have themselves dumbed down to the point that few college graduates today could pass tests given to eight-graders in the early 1800s.

"What is really needed is a genuine debate about education. Do not confuse education with the public-education industry. The oldest trick in the book used by those with a vested interest is to narrow the debate to tinkering with the status quo. That's what politicians are doing today."

11. Professional Programs

"Professional" is a greatly overused word these days. There are professional golfers, hairdressers, manicurists and lawn maintenance specialists. The classical interpretation would tend to limit the use of the word to those who, by their education, training, and supervised experience, qualify to perform a service upon receiving a license from the state. One debatable qualification is that they provide their services directly to the people, as opposed to working for an organization. Architects, for example, are very keen on this. They never work as an employee of a company, at least on the surface. Some critics say engineers are not professionals because they do not sell their services directly to the public, they tend to be employed by corporations or public bodies. But will a physician employed at a hospital lose his or her professional standing by working for a paycheck? Of course not.

The obvious candidates to the title of "professional" are those who, after receiving a bachelor's degree, complete a graduate education program leading to a "first professional degree." The minimum requirement for such a degree is six years of academic work, including the undergraduate course work. There are ten such degrees in the United States:

- Chiropractic (D.C. Or D.C.M.)
- Dentistry (D.S.S. Or D.M.D.)
- Law (LL.B. Or J.D.)
- Medicine (M.D.)
- Optometry (O.D.)
- Osteopathic Medicine (O.D.)

- Pharmacy (Pharm. D.)
- Podiatry (D.P.M., D.P., or Pod. D.)
- Theology (M. Div., M.H.L., B.D., or Ordination)
- Veterinary Medicine (D.V.M.)

In 1996, a total of 76,734 such degrees was awarded in the United States. The majority of these were law degrees, 39,828. The second largest group was the M.D.s: 15,341, then dentists: 3,697.

In comparison, 37,976 Ph.D. degrees were awarded in the same year, not counting degrees in education. Interestingly, when asked in a telephone survey, 44 percent of holders of first professional doctor's degrees claimed they have a Ph.D., which, in fact, was incorrect[1]. A law degree requires three years of study, while the average Ph.D. takes over seven years of graduate school. Another tidbit: in the 1960s many law schools changed their degrees retroactively from LL.B. (Bachelor of Laws) to J.D. (Juris Doctor). Federal government lawyers received an automatic raise. Such is the aura of a doctorate...

Another group of professionals obtain their "first professional degrees" when they finish an undergraduate program. Engineers, business majors, nurses and others are in this category.

Undergraduate professional programs' curricular requirements are slightly different from school to school.

1   *The New College Course Map and Transcript Files*, 2nd Ed., U.S. Dept. Of Education, 1999. p. 206.

Compared to other undergraduate degree requirements, they tend to be highly regimented and comparatively tough. The following examples were taken from a typical comprehensive state university. Three disciplines will be discussed: business administration, nursing and engineering. Each of of these degrees, upon completion of a bachelor degree and a certain number of years of supervised experience and the passing of a state examination, leads to professional licensing by a state.

This chapter is included to accentuate the fact that curricula leading to professional — and some other — disciplines include a highly organized set of courses that must be taken sequentially. This calls for a great deal of focusing and concentration by the student. Straying from the prescribed course of study to take some unrelated elective — regardless of how interesting it may appear — could be ruinous later. There is virtually no slack in these programs; one must stick to them closely to succeed.

After completing the first two or three semesters, university students apply for admission to the college of the discipline they are interested in. By the time of admission, often they have to have certain courses completed that the college prescribes. In the case of a typical College of Business Administration, the entrance requirements include a few Sophomore level courses such as Business Mathematics, Accounting Principles, or perhaps Behavioral Science. The business college also requires a minimum acceptable overall grade point average, for example 2.3 in a minimum of 40 credits taken before admission. With this requirement, the business faculty assure that they do not have to deal with students of academically inferior quality.

In most colleges of business, students must select a sub-discipline from a list of majors. These include Accounting, Advertising, Business Administration, Finance, International Business, Management, Marketing and Sales.

There is a core program required of all business administration students, in addition to individual departmental requirements for the sub-disciplines listed above. The core program generally contains a list of courses that add up to about 13 courses totaling 39 credits. In addition the students are required to take courses from the different departments of the business college, this may add up to an additional 24 credits. This latter requirement is designed to expose the student to the various disciplines outside of his or her specialty. There are variations between departmental requirements. For example, the core requirement for a degree in Accounting may be as much as 34 credits. This requirement is often prescribed by forces outside of academia. They are set, for instance, as academic requirements for those who wish to take the Uniform Certified Public Accounting Examination, the national qualifying examination for CPA status.

In general, a degree in business administration requires more than the commonly expected 120 credits for graduation. One typical overall requirement is 128 credits. Another requirement for graduation may be that a certain number, say 50 percent, of the total graduation credit requirement must be from outside of the college of business. This assures that the student has a solid exposure to non-business subjects. Of course, the General Education Requirements largely fulfill this demand.

The accrediting agency of colleges of business administration is the American Assembly of Collegiate Schools of Business. There are no more than a couple of hundred schools in the nation with such accreditation. A student interested in a business-oriented education should ascertain that the school considered has an accredited program, not just any program in business administration. Admission to graduate school, to obtain a coveted MBA, the Master of Business Administration degree, usually depends on having a fully accredited bachelor's degree. As in most respectable bachelor degree programs, some courses are more advanced than others. When selecting the courses, the student must observe the so called prerequisites. As an example, let us consider a senior business course called Marketing Strategy. It is preceded by Marketing Research, which in turn is preceded by Quantitative Business Analysis, that is preceded by College Algebra. These four courses, to be taken in sequence, amount to two years of study – providing that the courses are offered in subsequent semesters convenient for the student. It is not always so. A student who is off the regular cycle may have to wait a semester to get to the next course. The consequence of all this is that if a student flip-flops around in various courses and fields rather than consciously sticking to a program of study, finishing in four years will be doubtful. Graduation one year later than really necessary on account of some missed departmental course requirement could be expensive in time and money.

One of the toughest fields within business administration is accounting. To take the CPA examination one requires an undergraduate degree and two years of experience. While it is a lucrative profession, enrollment in accountancy has declined on college campuses recently. Perhaps the field is hurt by the nineteenth century Dickensian image of the green eyeshade, high stool and quill pen, but this is the age of computer spreadsheets and Hewlett-Packard business calculators. In 1997 15 percent fewer people have taken the national CPA examination than in 1990. This is a striking number in light of the fact that the number of public corporations has increased 20 percent in the past decade. Meanwhile the number of certified accountants in the United States remains almost steady at about 131,000. Stockholders of risk-taking companies need qualified accountants to scrutinize the books of their corporations. Since the Great Depression, every public corporation is required to hire outside auditors to review financial reports provided to stockholders by corporate executives. One of the incentives the accounting profession is trying to introduce to change their image is the concept that an accountant is not a bean counter but a certified financial advisor.

Another professional curriculum is offered by colleges of Nursing. Nursing programs are accredited by the National League for Nursing Accreditation Commission (NLNAC).

Admission to a nursing college, leading to a Bachelor of Science in Nursing, happens upon completion of the freshman year. However, even the curriculum of the freshman year is rigidly prescribed: a course in Biochemistry and one in Microbiology is required.

Admission to a nursing program is even tougher than admission to business administration. A typical college requires a minimum of a 2.5 overall grade point average at the time of admission. However, this is not a sufficient condition for entry. One college reviewed here has limited the number of admitted students to 160. Applicants starting from the highest overall GPA are admitted until the class is full.

Once admitted, nursing students follow a rigidly prescribed program. A rather unique and tough requirement in the program is that senior level courses can be taken only when *all* junior level requirements are fulfilled. The same goes for junior level courses: all sophomore requirements must have been completed.

In the Sophomore year, nurses study Anatomy, Physiology, Developmental Psychology and Statistics in four-credit courses offered by the respective academic departments. The rest of their academic work consists of nursing-related courses, for 15 credits. In the Junior year the work is even more intensive. It is spent entirely on courses about nursing, 34 credits of it. It is a particularly difficult year. In the Senior year 23 credits are in nursing; the rest of the load is used to cover General Education requirements. Overall, there is virtually no time available for a nursing student to elect a course for her special interest.

There is no slack in a nurse's education but the rewards are worth it. Having a bachelor's degree in nursing assures a person instant employment at any place in the country. There are over 600 bachelor level nursing schools in America, enrolling over 63,000 students. During the last five years of the 1990s enrollment declined by about 17 percent. This is probably caused by the fear that managed health care's concern about costs will result in reducing the number of nurses employed by hospitals and nursing homes. Meanwhile the average age of the U.S. population increases. The demand for registered nurses will grow by 21 percent by 2006 according to the U.S. Bureau of Labor Statistics. As medical care is the single largest business today in the United States, nurses with bachelor and masters degrees will be in demand for managerial positions at nursing homes, health maintenance organizations and hospitals.

Understaffed hospitals, overload and inadequate supervision of nurses caused 1,720 deaths and 9,548 injuries in the nation's hospitals between 1995 and 2000 according to a study of 3 million state and federal records conducted by the *Chicago Tribune*[2]. The records included cases of patients getting overdoses of medicine, vital care delayed for hours, and nurses performing medical procedures without proper training. Deadly mistakes by nurses are dwarfed by fatal mistakes by doctors. According to a 1999 report by the Institute of Medicine, medical mistakes kill anywhere from 44,000 to 98,000 hospitalized Americans each year, wrote the *Tribune*.

The third professional curriculum reviewed is offered by a College of Engineering. All engineering degrees are accredited by ABET, the Accrediting Board for Engineering and Technology. ABET is set up as a cooperative venture of a multitude of engineering professional associations covering a wide area of engineering specialties, like ASCE, ASME, IEEE, etc., representing civil, mechanical, electrical and other engineering specialties. Traditionally, the four main engineering specialties are mechanical, civil, chemical and electrical engineering. At large universities there are many other specialties, such as agricultural, coastal, computer, aeronautical and other engineering fields. Having only the four fundamental specialties available is not really a disadvantage. Specialization is best done at the graduate level.

There are fewer than 250 universities in America which offer accredited degrees in engineering. A new engineering

2   *Chicago Tribune*, September 10, 2000

program can not be accredited until it actually has graduates: therefore there is a small window when a few graduates, at least temporarily, have no accredited degrees. Aside from such cases, enrolling to an engineering program with no ABET accreditation is not advisable.

Engineering is a financially rewarding career. According to a 1998 survey by the American Association of Engineering Societies a typical engineer with 14 years of experience in industry earned $ 64,500 in a year, not bad for a profession that requires no more than a four-year college education.

The national accreditation requirements for a bachelor degree in engineering, prescribed by ABET, are as follows:

One year of mathematics and basic science, [Note: pre-calculus mathematics courses do not count.] and one year of engineering science, one-half year of engineering design, and one-half year of humanities and social sciences.

These requirements are on the top of the university's General Education Requirements, although reduced to 29 credits. The last requirement, courses in humanities and social sciences, is quite ridiculous. For a professional accreditation agency to insist on a whole semester of course-work that has nothing to do with the profession is frivolous. Whether it stems from an innate atavistic inferiority complex of the artisan with respect to the humanists, or sheer hypocrisy, one cannot know. Perhaps the engineers want to convince the liberal arts crowd that they should include in their curriculum some courses in science also. But why do they bother, at the expense of their already overloaded engineering students?

Admission to the College of Engineering requires that the student at the time of application have completed 30 credits with a GPA of 2.3 in three of the following four groups of courses: engineering, mathematics, science, and all courses taken. This makes freshmen who intend to apply to the engineering college quite busy. Over one in two of those who originally planned to enter never make it.

Within the college of engineering, each department has its requirements. As an example, let us take the Department of Civil Engineering. This engineering specialty encompasses various fields such as geotechnical, environmental, hydraulic, structural and transportation engineering. While all are civil engineers, their fields are far enough apart to cause communication difficulties between them.

The civil engineering departmental requirements call for a core courses in engineering science — Statics, Fluid Dynamics, and the like — all together amounting to a minimum of 24 credits.

In addition to the engineering science core mentioned above, there is an applied civil engineering core. It ranges from courses like Theory of Structures and Construction Administration, totaling 38 credits. For specialization within the department, 12 credits of civil engineering electives at senior level are required from a rather narrow list of courses that are offered.

The total graduation requirement for a degree in engineering at a typical engineering college is 137 semester credits. The general education requirements, engineering science core, the departmental core and the required electives total 103 credits. The remainder are 34 credits, or about eleven courses during the four year program of an engineer, that are to be taken as true electives. Most students elect courses from related disciplines, such as mathematics, geology, or another specialty of engineering.

One of the difficulties of all engineering curricula is the unusual length of prerequisite chains. The advanced mathematics requirement, for instance, assumes that the student already completed Differential Equations, the basic tool of mathematics to solve problems of engineering physics. Newton's laws of motion, for instance, require such mathematics knowledge. This course, however, must be preceded by three semesters of Calculus. To take Calculus I, one must have the prerequisite courses in Trigonometry and Algebra, a tall order for most graduates of public high-schools. Even if these two are taken in the same semester, the prerequisite chain to get to the senior level mathematics requirement takes five semesters, two and a half years of academic work.

An undergraduate degree in any field of engineering is one of the best academic investments. While some engineering schools, like MIT, Caltech and others have stellar reputations, generally engineering programs are standardized to such a degree that there is precious little difference in the material learned from one school to another. Typically, engineering textbooks for most engineering courses offered are limited to one or two popular titles. Hence most schools use identical textbooks. As engineering professors usually are graduates of large research universities, there is little difference in their training. This suggests that a degree in engineering from any accredited school is a bargain among bachelor degrees.

Production of undergraduate engineers in American universities has fallen almost 20 percent since 1986, according to the American Association of Engineering Societies. This bit of statistical data is particularly interesting if we consider that overall production of bachelor degrees in general has increased 18 percent in the same time period.

One of the problems engineering schools face in America is the lack of popularity the field enjoys among women. A 1998 Lou Harris poll has shown that 78 percent of women were uninformed about the fields of engineering.

Feminist legislators' efforts to force the Navy to allow women to serve on submarines would be much better spent on convincing girls to study engineering. The once formidable U.S. Navy has already succumbed to the feminists in allowing female sailors on surface ships. According to a September 2000 *Associated Press* report, heads will be replaced by unisex toilets on Navy ships. The cost of installing a single unisex toilet in an aircraft carrier would pay the cost of two females' tuition, room and board while studying at MIT for four years. By promoting engineering education for girls, America's ardent feminist congresswomen and senators could provide themselves more impressive — if not more fitting — memorials than stainless steel toilets.

Women's lack of interest in engineering in general is in marked contrast with the success of female engineering students and female engineering graduates. Experience shows that female engineering students are in the middle to the top of their classes academically. Opinions among engineering professors in regard to women's better-than-average performance varies. Some say that women are better at details, which makes them excel in engineering. Others are of the opinion that women students work harder because they feel that they must prove themselves in a "masculine field." Old conventions and views concerning the macho appeal of engineering notwithstanding, today's engineering is gender-neutral. A micro-processor manufacturing facility, a fab, is about as space-age as it gets. There is little muddy boot, rough and ready macho engineering anymore. Pecking away at the keyboard of a computer work station does not exactly have the nimbus of the Marlboro man, a the proverbial glass ceilings do not exist, except in the delirious imagination of feminist zealots.

To break the stigma, the alleged gender-barrier of engineering, Smith College, one of the paradigms of women's colleges, decided in 1999 to establish an engineering program. With the constant demand for more engineers in American industry, it was a wise choice.

Professional life is tough on women. Former female students of this writer have reached high engineering managerial positions in state government alongside being mothers. But two females in one particular year had to drop out of their doctoral programs when faced with the parallel demands of being mothers.

Women in medicine experience identical problems. They account for about 45 percent of medical students today, up from 25 percent twenty years ago, but in taking time off for child rearing, they sacrifice higher salaries in fields that demand additional medical education. They select professional fields that allow working hours from 9 AM to 5 PM. According to a recent study, 25 percent of female doctors worked fewer than 40 hours a week. In comparison, only 8 percent of male doctors work fewer than 40 hours a week. As a result in the year 1998 a male doctor in private practice made over $ 273,000, compared to $ 155,000 for female practitioners. Combining a demanding profession with family life is a difficult challenge women face.

12. Going to College

More than one among four high school graduates elects to go to college. They are offered a great variety of services to select the "most appropriate" academic program at the "best schools." They should be wary and cautious when receiving such help. As outlined in the previous pages, the choices are critical.

Prospective college students receive a flood of advice from high school guidance counselors and college admissions officers. Mostly, the advice stresses two primary issues: what would you like to study? — and how to get into the college that is *best* for you. Best, of course is essentially depends on the subject matter the student wants to study. But little effort is put into explaining to the student that the choice of a field of study is essentially a lifelong career choice with serious professional and economic implications. Going to college is not part of a transient experience of growing up, before easing into "real life," a last dance before the ball of childhood is over. It is the first step of a life-long career.

It is human nature that parents would like to stretch out this period of separation, but by choosing the *best* school — a cute little liberal arts college offering a pre-Jacksonian curriculum — allegedly designed to develop the students' analytical capability, boasting, for instance, a superlative music conservatory and independent research opportunities — parents are not investing wisely in their child's future. If he or she is not ready for the real world, it is better to stay home, and perhaps learn a trade, make a little money working at K-Mart, join the Marines — grow up. If he or she is ready for college, then aim for the schools where the professional opportunities are the greatest and the offerings are the broadest. Why go to 7-Eleven if it is just as convenient to go to Wal-Mart?

Small colleges that fancy themselves "elite schools," offering a "broad-based" liberal arts education, quite often offer little learning that could keep their graduates out of the poor house. A graduate of one of the Midwest's small but nationally recognized "classy" private colleges completed several courses of great social import, such as South American liberation theology, as part of her graduation requirement. After graduation, however, she found no other employment opportunity beyond working as an assistant at a kindergarten. Having made a decision to work for a master's degree in Physical Therapy, she found that she lacks the required undergraduate preparation in mathematics and chemistry. It took two full years of make-up work, including summer sessions, to became qualified for graduate school. After she was finally admitted, finishing the graduate program took two additional years. Eight years for a master's degree! With a bit of planning before college, and less concern with "class," she could have had a doctorate in some worthy field in the same time period.

Another small private college, this one located in the Southeast, admitted a freshman into their "unique" curriculum that ostensibly led toward a job in the Diplomatic Service of the U. S. State Department. During Christmas break of the junior year, the school even arranged a field trip to Washington D.C. to visit the State Department, the students' alleged future stomping ground. At the end of all this, the student was issued a B.A. in History, qualifying him for an unpaid internship at a local library. Two years of graduate study and some $ 24,000 later he finally obtained a M.A. in Library Science which led to a fine position. This is a story of outright collegiate fraud. The graduates of this "unique" program were not advised during their four-year education that:

- the U.S. State Department offers the Foreign Service Examination once a year throughout the country;
- there are over 20,000 people taking the examination every year;
- only about 200 or so applicants are admitted each year into the Diplomatic Service; and
- the average age of people entering the State Department is over 28 years.

What is particularly interesting about these two cases that all four parents involved are college educated, both fathers have advanced degrees in engineering, and they both earn over $ 100,000 year. Apparently they paid less attention to their children's college education than one spends on buying a new refrigerator.

While the United States is the ultimate of the world's consumer societies, we seem totally to disregard colleges as purveyors of value. A student will cheerfully pay $ 100,000 for a bachelor's degree in social studies from a hyped up ivy-covered small college, when a degree in business administration or computer engineering from a major red-brick-and-concrete state university with immensely more massive educational facilities can be had for $40,000.

But the consumers — parents and students — appear to think that college life is as they have seen it in old movies. They dream of pristine scenes around ivy-covered walls, wise old professors instilling age-old values in their students' fertile mind. In many of our liberal arts colleges, quite the opposite is the case. As has just been demonstrated, only the professional curricula are relatively safe.

There is just too much required course work in undergraduate professional programs to force in additional elective
courses, stuff that includes the discredited socialist dogma.
There are a few feminist "nutty professors" around who
would be ready and willing to insert "feminist viewpoints"
into science courses, but so far bridges, for instance, are designed for strength rather than for feelings.

There are many "consultants" who make their living out of
testing students inclinations, intellectual and artistic capa-
bilities, likes and dislikes, dispensing advice on the selection of careers. Psychologists use various sorts of
computerized testing programs that supposedly determine
the best career choice for a young person, discovering the
best match of their personality types to over 1,500 occupational possibilities. Some of these tests may be helpful, but
they require a professional to administer them. Personality
inventory tests, for example, may determine that one has a
remarkable mathematical aptitude, coupled with a love of
music. Consequently, it may recommend a career in accounting followed by work at the business office of the
Cleveland Orchestra.

Career guidance counselors are at hand in high schools.
They do provide a service, but only to a point. The all appear to disregard the essential economic questions. How
well do you want to live once you get your diploma? Would
you like to be able to support a family with the knowledge
you gain in college?

It is really up to the individual to find his or her place in life.
No outside assistance can replace a thorough self-assess-
ment and self-directed search for a suitable career. In the
twenty-first century, one can expect several mid-life career
changes as life-style and technology change in an ever increasing rate. Hence, one must be prepared for new oppor-

tunities, for drastic change. One must, therefore, take the hard stuff at college, and even in high school — otherwise a person will be at a disadvantage throughout his or her working life.

Even if a person's goals are set at a high level, what one does at the undergraduate school is not only important, it can be decisive. Let's say the goal is a law degree. It may be suggested, for instance, that an undergraduate degree in accounting would be a better choice than some committee of college professors' idea of what constitutes a pre-law preparation. The difference could thwart one's admission to law school. Furthermore, a strong, economically viable undergraduate degree will always be a useful thing to fall back on, if one's law school admission is denied. The same goes for medicine. To become a doctor, for example, a Bachelor of Science in Chemistry would be a useful beginning.

Even though a person may have glorious plans for an eventual professional, advanced degree, the fact is that 79 percent of bachelor degree holders never attempt graduate education.[1]

There really are two choices, once the decision for college is made. One path is to work on a degree that can be utilized in four years of rather intensive study and another two to four of professional practice. Another path is to take four years of preparatory undergraduate work immediately fol-

---

1   *Life after College, a Descriptive Summary of 1992-93 Bachelor's Degree Recipients in 1997,* National Center of Educational Statistics, Statistical Analysis Report, June 1999.

lowed by another program that leads to a professional degree, law, dentistry, psychology, medicine and others.

Unless one of these goals is set before the whole college program is started, there will be years of academic work wasted, years spent without any discernible advance, a lot of money misspent and other potential opportunities missed. Going to a college that offers nothing but a liberal arts education — just because a student has not made up his or her mind about a career — is not a wise choice. It is the mariner's problem: "When one doesn't know which way to sail, no wind is favorable."

Graduating high school students are bewildered by the enormous choice of training and employment opportunities, trades and professions available to them. Many, however, see only a limited number of role models they may or may not wish to emulate. A kid growing up on a farm is likely to know a veterinarian, but never see an advertising executive. A city-dweller is similarly handicapped when it comes to work opportunities in the countryside. Reading, talking to a great variety of people with different experiences and networking will help to broaden one's outlook. Selecting a suitable profession, defining a focus is far more important than picking a college.

Bookstore shelves and guidance counselors' offices are full of such information. One of the best sources is offered by the federal government. Every year the U.S. Bureau of Labor Statistics releases its *Occupational Outlook Handbook* which is by far the most authoritative source of information. Not only does it present hundreds of descriptions of what a particular occupation entails, it also provides detailed data on expected earnings and the professional expectations for the next several years. For each type of employment the Handbook describes the nature of the work, working conditions, key industries employing workers in each type of occupation, training and other necessary qualifications, advancement potentials, job outlook in future years, the degree of competition, earnings potential and related occupations. It also provides a listing for associations, government agencies and other organizations which provide useful additional information. One may purchase a copy at a bookstore, or read it on-line at their website:

http://www.bls.gov/ocohome.htm

Another useful on-line information source on careers is the *Dow Jones* website:

http://dowjones.com/careers

Likewise, the *Wall Street Journal*'s website is also very informative

http://careers.wsj.com

It provides employment profiles and salaries culled from the *National Business Employment Weekly* magazine.

Once a person identifies a potential career choice, the time for selecting colleges has arrived. First, it is advisable to review the whole market without regard to geography. It is nice to know what is available before one selects a school that would fill the same need at a more convenient location.

There are several outstanding publications that provide information about most of these schools. One of the best, Barron's *Profiles of American Colleges* must be in the hand of any high-school student who considers going to college. Among the most important information these profiles contain is the status of accreditation of a college and its various disciplines.

To find out all about colleges and universities in America, by far the best source is found on the Internet. A consortium of several outstanding universities created *CollegeEdge* that allows anyone interested to get highly detailed information on over 6,000 higher education institutions, free of charge. Selection of schools by fields of specialty — ranging in fields from agriculture to veterinary science — is also available. Applications can be submitted on line and information is passed on to university recruiters to how to contact the potential applicant. This jewel of a tool is found at

http://excite.collegeedge.com/main/colledgeedge.asp

This source also provides an unexpectedly huge body of information about class sizes, the holdings of the library and a great deal of other stuff that can be used to compare one school to another.

Another excellent Internet website, *CollegeNET,* helps find the "ideal" college, grouped by region, providing information on majors offered, sports, tuition and so on is at

http://www.collegeNET.com

A great deal could be learned about a lot of American campuses by reading the campus papers on-line. There is plenty of unvarnished information about the colleges contained in them. Many could be accessed through the *Collegiate Network*

http://www.isi.org/cn/links2.html

With the aid of books, magazine reports, Internet resources and information supplied by the admission offices, the prospective student will be able to determine where are best places in the United States to acquire the knowledge desired, where are the universities that offer the best programs.

One of the problems students face in getting a degree is the growing cost of college education. In 1998 the increase of tuition and fees was twice the rate of inflation. In public institutions the tuition has risen 50 percent in the past ten years, while family income went up 1.5 percent. Tuition assistance in the form of grants and loans helps partly to alleviate the problem. In 1998 some $ 60 billion was available for college students in the United States. Sadly, much of it is in the form of loans, not in the form of grants. Today, 60 percent of the available financial aid is loans, up from 40 percent from some 20 years ago. This places a serious burden on graduating students. Many accumulate debts, as much as $ 10,000, before graduation. The average debt of a medical school graduate in 1999 was $ 90,000. Even greater burden is placed on those students who receive the loans but do not stay until graduation. They are left with a burden of a loan that often they can not repay.

But going to school full-time is not the only way. "The system of higher education is really two systems. There is a parent-pulverizing full-time four-year college system (as much as $ 100,000 to get a bachelor's degree at Stanford, not counting room and board; $ 40,000 at the University of California). And there is the cost effective part-time system. That might cost a person $ 12,000 for a bachelor's degree over eight years and wouldn't keep one out of the labor force. In a profound shift since the 1960s, American students have significantly opted for the latter," reported *Forbes* magazine.

Particularly hurt are the low income families. To attend a public, four-year university, a low income family has to fork over 62 percent of its yearly income. A middle class family needs to spend only 17 percent of its income for the same. Federal Pell grants, the major funding source for low income students, declined 23 percent over the past 20 years when adjusted for inflation. Meanwhile college costs have risen 49 percent in the same period. In 1998 the maximum Pell grant was $ 3,000 a year. Congress is considering raising this limit, but not by a significant amount. Of the 15 million students in America's campuses about 3.6 million qualify for Pell grants. More than half of these qualify for the full amount. This compares poorly with the cost of education. In the school year 1995-96 the average cost of a public four-year university was $ 10,889. In the same year a four-year private university charged $ 19,443 according to the American Council on Education. The average cost for a full time student without financial aid at a two-year college was $ 7,265. That is a lot of money for a low income family.

Various other federally funded grants are also available. Supplemental Educational Opportunity grants, as well as Pell grants are subject to a congressionally prescribed Expected Family Contribution (EFC), the money the student's family supposed to pay. For low income students the Federal Government, as well as many state governments, offer a variety of low cost, subsidized loans. Stafford, PLUS, Consolidation and Perkins loans are federally funded. Many of these are offered regardless of family income level. In addition, many schools offer loans through arrangements with local financial institutions.

Scholarships are another potential funding sources for college. The really good ones are scarce. Still it is worthwhile to look into this possibility. A helpful Internet aid in researching over 400,000 scholarships is

Unfortunately, many scholarships listed are either too insignificant or overly restricted. Few applicants will qualify for a $ 500 a year memorial scholarship under the condition that one must have been born in Barberton, Ohio, to ethnic Albanian parents. While this is a fictional example, college financial aids officers can bring up many such cases.

Students can obtain merit aid at some schools where their class rank and test scores place them in the top 25 percent of the applicant pool. The most generous colleges tend to be second-tier private schools that boast large endowments but face stiff competition from academically comparable state schools. Carnegie-Mellon, for instance, is one example. The University of Pittsburgh is across the street. Students could apply to competing schools and play them off against each other. One may offer extra money to attract a student from the other school. Merit scholarships, as opposed to needs-based ones, are on the rise nationwide.

Some universities offer Cooperative Work-Study programs. There is even a federal work-study program available. The real "co-op" programs are the "classical" ones originally started some 80 years ago at schools like the University of Cincinnati, Northeastern University, the University of Akron and some others. These programs are built on close cooperation with participating industry and governmental agencies. The essence of these programs is the expansion of the junior year to two calendar years, during which the student alternates between working a semester in industry under carefully controlled conditions and attending college for a semester. Upon graduation the student has a whole year of industrial experience which may, or may not, lead to a job offer from the cooperating firm. Supporters of the co-op program point out that upon completing the sophomore year, the co-op student will have stronger finances to complete his or her degree and will have added maturity at the time of graduation. Opponents note that the student will have a degree one year later, a year that could be spent on making money, learning a foreign language or on other beneficial endeavors.

For financially better-off parents, college savings plans were made recently available in several states. They allow tax-deferred savings up to about $ 100,000 for each child's college expenses. The money is invested under the state's supervision into stocks, bonds and money market funds, and are operated under the Internal Revenue Service Code Rule 529. All of these mean that the investment will minimize risk. They also insure the investor against raises of tuition. Compared to a straight investment into mutual funds, these college savings plans are not much of a bargain. Early withdrawal for non-educational spending brings about a ten percent penalty. Another shortcoming of these state-controlled college investments is that the funds are to be spent within the state. This may not be convenient for some who would prefer an out-of-state college. The definite advantage of these programs is that they encourage families to start their planning early and save consistently long before the bills start coming in.

An interesting glimpse is provided into goings-on at admissions offices at selective colleges — well, at least at Dartmouth College — in a book by Hernandez[2]. She

2   Michele A. Hernandez: *A Is for Admission: The Insider's Guide to Getting Into the Ivy League and Other Top Colleges*, Warner Books, 1997.

worked at Dartmouth's admissions office for a while and presents her experiences as "one of America's most guarded secrets." She reports that only 60 percent of Dartmouth's students are admitted "entirely on their academic merit," that grades are really not as important as the various test scores, that the application deadline isn't really a deadline, that blacks are twice as likely as white applicants to be admitted, and that the waiting list is a charade. Admissions officers at Ivy League colleges probably raise an issue about some of the book's arguments. They are paid to do it. But the fact is that admissions selectivity is not only matter of merit, but also a combination of hype and social engineering.

What are the chances to get in? Regardless what one wants to study and where one wants to do that, the better high school grades are, the greater are the chances of admission. Interestingly, the number one concern of college faculty, the greatest obstacle to their work, is the lack of preparation and commitment of their students[3]. Over 50 percent of polled faculty members claimed this to be their main concern.

A few decades ago one of the respected Midwestern universities made a study of their graduates' success in life. High-school grades, GPA's at graduation and all other likely predictors were compared. The most reliable factor turned out to be the height of the graduates. Taller people were more successful in life than others. So much for celebrating diversity.

3   The American Faculty Poll, *The Chronicle of Higher Education*, March 3, 2000.

What courses one takes in high school has a great deal to do with later success. Mathematics is the best predictor. Having good math skills will help a lot. Not having much will severely limit one's future options. With normal intelligence, there is no such thing as lack of talent in mathematics. Only the lack of good mathematics teachers, lack of diligence, lack of focus, and lack of persistence can keep one from obtaining the necessary mathematics skills. According to federal statistics[4] of students whose highest mathematics course in high school was pre-algebra only 2.3 percent earned a Bachelor's degree. On the other hand 79.8 percent of those who took a course in calculus in high school earned one.

If one comes right down to it, the more prestigious a field of study, the more mathematics is involved in learning it. One could never make it through medical school without knowing biochemistry and organic chemistry. Without mathematics skills, one will never make it through those courses. MBAs carry their Hewlett-Packard calculators like preachers carry their Bibles. Making business decisions without mathematical calculations would be madness. Even an M.S. degree in Physical Therapy has all sorts of chemistry and mathematics course requirements.

According to the year 2000 edition of the *Jobs Rated Almanac*[5], based on statistical data from the U. S. Department of

<hr>

4   National Center of Educational Statistics: *High-school and Beyond/Sophomore Cohort*, 1982-1993.

5   Les Krantz: *Jobs Rated Almanac*, St. Martin's Griffin, 2000.

Labor, the top ten jobs among the 250 ranked were all in mathematics and computer related fields.

Lack of mathematics preparation should not prevent a college-bound student from achieving his or her life goals. If one's high-school preparation was inadequate to such a degree that admission to the "right" college program is unlikely, it is advisable to take off a year and concentrate on mathematics at a nearby community or technical college. Once one shows up with a batch of college-level mathematics courses passed with flying colors, admissions officers will be impressed.

Another highly important asset is communication skills. Psychological studies show that vocabulary is the best predictor of high intelligence. Reading builds vocabulary. It should start early. Unfortunately, many Americans have atrocious reading skills, even though there is no other country on earth with so many libraries and so many books sold than the United States. Buying a good dictionary and getting a library card is a cheap and effective way to start someone off in the right direction.

Many liberal arts graduates found their writing skills their sole salvation on the marketplace. Even the most advanced Silicon Valley high-tech firms need people who write well. Communicating well is crucial in business. Big corporations spend tens of millions of dollars each year on outside talent — advertising agencies — to make sure their message is conveyed well. A college-bound student's application letter or essay is his or her advertisement. At the least, it better not have spelling errors.

Good writing skills are very important. So is coherent speech. Recognizing the problem of having a generation of speech-challenged students, M.I.T., Mount Holyoke, Holy

Cross and Wesleyan colleges initiated programs recently on "Speaking, Arguing and Writing," emphasizing oral presentations. The thought is that "if the students have something to say, they are going to be able to say it well." Fifty years ago, Tom Lehrer, Harvard math professor turned humorist/singer, put it well: "If you can't communicate, the least you can do is shut up."

Among extracurricular activities in high-school, nothing makes a college admissions officer salivate more than athletics. Athletics directors clamor for new talents for their teams, a sizeable portion of the scholarship money is set aside to support new recruits. But to be a college athlete or to follow a rigorous academic program are often mutually exclusive activities. Business administration, engineering and similar studies particularly do not mix well with athletics. Regardless, getting into college with an athletic scholarship is great, if that is one's only choice.

Some colleges appear to give a lot of weight to the applicant's "activities" in high school outside of the classroom. They want "well rounded" individuals. This may give the impression that nerds are not welcome. Bill Gates was a nerd. So was Steven Jobs. Both did all right. Larger schools put a great deal less weight on such personal matters. Being a social busybody in high school is not a predictor of collegiate success.

Note on URL's

The Internet websites given in the text were carefully checked before the book was sent to the printer. They all worked. However, it was found that while some sites could be entered directly after typing in the whole address, others worked only when at first only the primary domain address was put in, followed by the rest in a step by step manner.

Most of the sites, by the way, are really great.

Other books by Andrew L. Simon

Books Authored:

Energy Resources, Pergamon Press, 1975

Practical Hydraulics, Wiley, 1976

Basic Hydraulics, Wiley, 1983

Principles of Statics and Strength of Materials, West, 1983

Fire Hydraulics, Prentice Hall, 1983

Hydraulics, 2e, Prentice Hall, 1996

Made in Hungary, Simon Publ., 1999

Books Edited:

Admiral Nicholas Horthy: **Memoirs**

H.H. Bandholtz: **An Undiplomatic Diary**

Imre Josika-Herczeg; **Hungary after a Thousand Years**

Matatias Carp: **Holocaust in Romania**

Oscar Halecki: **Borderlands of Western Civilization**